Spirituality
and
Pastoral Care

THEOLOGY AND PASTORAL CARE SERIES

edited by
Don S. Browning

Life Cycle Theory and Pastoral Care
  by Donald Capps

Religious Ethics and Pastoral Care
  by Don S. Browning

A Roman Catholic Theology of Pastoral Care
  by Regis A. Duffy, O.F.M.

The Family and Pastoral Care
  by Herbert Anderson

Care of Souls in the Classic Tradition
  by Thomas C. Oden

Pastoral Care and Hermeneutics
  by Donald Capps

Pastoral Care and the Jewish Tradition
  by Robert L. Katz

Professionalism and Pastoral Care
  by Alastair V. Campbell

Spirituality and Pastoral Care
  by Nelson S. T. Thayer

NELSON S. T. THAYER

Spirituality and Pastoral Care

Don S. Browning, *editor*

THEOLOGY AND PASTORAL CARE

FORTRESS PRESS
PHILADELPHIA

Library of Congress Cataloging in Publication Data

Thayer, Nelson S. T.
  Spirituality and pastoral care.

  (Theology and pastoral care series)
  Includes bibliographical references.
  1. Spirituality.   2. Pastoral counseling.   3. Prayer.
I. Browning, Don S.   II. Title.   III. Series.
BV4509.5.T53   1985   253.5   84–48715
ISBN 0–8006–1734–7

1265A85   Printed in the United States of America   1–1734

Contents

Series Foreword   7

Preface   11

Introduction   13

1. The Cultural and Religious Context of
   Contemporary Pastoral Care   15

2. Spirituality and Spirit   31

3. A Theory of Pastoral Care   61

4. The Function of Prayer in Spiritual
   Formation   73

Notes   123

70968

Series Foreword

After decades of preoccupation on the part of both theologians and the church with representing the Christian faith as intellectually acceptable to the modern mind, recent years have witnessed a rediscovery of what is commonly called "spirituality." The term "spirituality" has a variety of meanings in the contemporary discussion, but in general it refers to that dimension of Christian living that emphasizes various disciplines and practices designed to deepen one's sense of being related to the divine. The historical trends leading to this new interest in Christian spirituality are still not fully understood. The quasi-religious altered states of consciousness experienced by young people dabbling with the drug culture in the 1960s and 1970s, the parallel discovery of Eastern mystical traditions, the widespread disillusionment with modern, technological, and scientific culture, and the pervasive sense of the loss of a sense of self-transcendence, however defined, have all worked together to create in many modern individuals the need to find significance in their lives through religious experience. One of the most outstanding achievements of contemporary religious scholarship has been the gradual unearthing and reappropriation of the spiritual tradition of both Christianity and Judaism. Nelson Thayer's book builds on this scholarship but also extends it.

For the past several years, Professor Thayer has been a pioneer in investigating the relation of spirituality to pastoral care. In his teaching at the Theological School of Drew University and within the context of numerous workshops held throughout the country, Nelson Thayer has developed a unique understanding of and approach to spirituality within the context of pastoral care. Spirituality, he tells us, does not just refer to inner subjective feelings, it has primarily to do with the total integration of life. It is the function of religion to integrate experience, and spirituality is the disciplined involvement with the divine toward the end of gathering together into a coherent whole the diverse facets of our ordinary experience.

Nelson Thayer places his interest in spirituality within the context of recent developments in philosophy that relativize positivistic science as the only approach to the acquisition of knowledge. It is now commonly acknowledged in philosophical circles that although the experimental sciences do provide us with certain important yet limited forms of knowledge, they should not be seen as exhausting all the forms of knowledge needed or available for human purposes. These philosophical discussions have had the effect of opening modern consciousness once again to a careful reconsideration of the forms of knowledge conveyed through spiritual experiences.

Central to all forms of spirituality is a process that Professor Thayer calls "centering." Centering is a disciplined yet relaxed focusing of attention on some aspect of our inner experience. Thayer artfully guides the reader through a variety of centering disciplines from elementary forms of breath-counting to discussions of the apophatic or consciousness-emptying traditions of the desert fathers, the Jesus Prayer, the Prayer of the Heart in the Greek Orthodox Church, the traditions associated with the classical *Cloud of Unknowing*, verbalizing forms of prayer, and the more imagistic forms of prayer. In these discussions the reader will be treated to a firm and balanced introduction to these traditions and a careful and sensible assessment of their proper place within the pastoral care of the congregation.

In *Spirituality and Pastoral Care,* Nelson Thayer has made a lasting contribution toward broadening and deepening our understanding of the full dimensions of pastoral care.

DON S. BROWNING

Preface

I am happy to express appreciation for companions on the way who by being themselves have deepened my understanding of spirituality and Spirit. Lawrence LeShan knows more about the problems and possibilities in being human than any person I have met. He and the other men and women of the Consciousness Research and Training Project, Inc. have, over the years, been a continuing community of illumination, healing, and hilarity.

The Reverend Joseph Cantillon, S.J., is a fearless son of the Church and a faithful father in God. His critical biblical understanding, commitment to social justice, devotion to the Trinity, and pleasure in being human incarnate holistic spiritual direction.

The Reverend James Kirby, Ph.D., and the Reverend Thomas Ogletree, Ph.D., as friends and deans, by word and deed have encouraged and supported my interest in spirituality.

It has been my privilege for many years to teach a year-long course in meditation and prayer at the Theological School of Drew University. Also, for several years I have been teaching week-long intensives for men and women in our Doctor of Ministry program. The participants in these projects range in age from twenty-three to sixty-five. With generosity, commitment, and skepticism, they have shared their experience and their thinking with me. I cannot conceive of having written this book without them.

I especially want to thank Jean Ruch, Connie McKenna, and Mitzi Pappas for their forbearance, good cheer, and mastery of the mysteries of word processing.

Although this book is written for Christian pastors and draws on the Christian tradition, it has been developed within an overall perspective that understands spirit as a human phenomenon and Spirit as a human symbol for a truth that manifests itself in many traditions, with many meanings. For more than two decades my wife, Mai Leung Thayer, and I have discussed these issues, and in our life together have shared their implications. To her the book is dedicated.

Introduction

Spirituality is an ambiguous subject. So fundamental to our being as humans, it nevertheless denies us the security of a circumscribed definition. In the most general sense, spirituality has to do with how we experience ourselves in relation to what we designate as the source of ultimate power and meaning in life, and how we live out this relationship. Spirituality is not merely inner feelings; it has to do with the integration and coherence of ourselves as experiencing and acting persons.

This book is especially intended for pastors whose understanding of the person has been informed to some extent by such teachers as Sigmund Freud, Erik Erikson, Carl Rogers, and Carl Jung, and who understand the importance of these perspectives for pastoral care and counseling. Such pastors tend to assume the developmental nature of the life cycle. But in recent years, these women and men have wanted a more specific linkage of such theory and practice to the more specifically religious dimensions of human experience and development. Such concern has grown out of their life experience, their experience as practitioners of pastoral care, their leadership of congregations, and their observation of the quality of contemporary culture. This book attempts to provide the theoretical linkage and to show how the practice of prayer functions in the overall dynamic of spirituality, and how this articulates with pastoral care as it has come to be practiced by a psychologically informed generation of clergy.

Liturgy, Christian education, preaching, structures of community and fellowship, social action, and charity are all formative and expressive of spirituality. Prayer and pastoral care occur in the context of these other essentials of Christian spirituality and are interdependent with them. The focus of this book on the relation of spirituality, prayer, and pastoral care is functional, not polemical over against these other spheres of spirituality.

Finally, in recent years there has developed an awareness of the distinctiveness of the spiritualities of various groupings, such as women, Asians, middle-aged male WASPS, blacks, Hispanics, and Native Americans. It is important to affirm the pursuit of such distinctiveness, and it is becoming increasingly possible to identify some of the elements of such distinctiveness. And yet the more deeply one participates in any given community, the more one is impressed not only by the distinctiveness of the group but also by the diversity within the distinctiveness. This makes one cautious lest characterization degenerate into stereotyping.

But what has emerged unequivocally from this pursuit of distinctive spiritualities is the recognition that spirituality is embodied, lived experience, influenced by historical, cultural, and social circumstances. There can be no one normative Christian spirituality. And while spirituality includes cognitive orientation, it transcends the intellect and is formed by and gives form to our relationships, our experience of our bodies, our commitments, our ecstasies, our aesthetics. It is hoped that the conceptual categories that follow are clear enough and at a sufficient level of generalization so as to include the widest possible range of spiritualities.

CHAPTER 1

The Cultural
and Religious Context
of Contemporary
Pastoral Care

Pastors serious about the relationship of spirituality and pastoral care want to know more than some techniques for making prayer less boring. A decade of teaching such pastors has shown that they realize spirituality is a fecund concept and that it goes to the heart of pastoral care. These men and women know that the concept seems at odds with much of what characterizes our culture, and that the concept carries one beyond the psychotherapeutic models that have dominated thinking about pastoral care for the past twenty years.

A book that attempts to treat the subject spirituality and pastoral care must take seriously the cultural context within which pastoral care occurs. Pastoral care does not occur in a vacuum, but within a matrix of social processes. How the pastor perceives, experiences, and evaluates these processes will affect both the actions of pastoral care and the overall "mood" in which pastoral care is carried out. Therefore, this book begins with a brief overview of what is perceived to be the current cultural context of pastoral care, and some observations about the implications for pastoral care.

Of course, the cultural context is not "one thing." Our culture is diverse, and any generalization about it can be met not only with a disproving example, but with a countergeneralization that is likely to be just as true. Nevertheless, there are some important characteristics that can be recognized.

First, and overarching, is the cultural phenomenon known as modernity. Modernity is characterized by the aggregate effect of the rise of modern science, technology, the differentiation of labor, secularization, and the loss of transcendence. The rise of modern science is by now a story well-known and need not be retold here. But its main elements need to be noted, for purposes of reminder and orientation.

Modern science is rooted in the empirical method of investigation which assumes that knowledge must be gained through the senses or their technological extensions, and that what is real is measurable and only that which is measurable is real. The so-called epistemological stance of modern science is the separation of knowing subject and known object. The assumption is that reality is knowable through the senses of the knowing subject.

The scientific method was to free knowing from the distortions of feelings and authority. Knowledge could be verified by replicable experiments and thereby validated consensually on the basis of objective evidence objectively observed and acquired. Again, the aim was to rule out the influences of individual predispositions and bias. The rise of modern science posed immense challenges to religion, in the work of Copernicus, Galileo, Darwin, and many others, whose discoveries were said to undermine the truth and authority of the religious tradition. The historical-critical approach to the Bible also was felt by many to pose a similar threat.

A major cultural effect of the rise of modern science has been secularization, which Peter Berger has defined as "the process by which sectors of society and culture are removed from the domination of religious institutions and symbols."[1]

He goes on to say that secularization "affects the totality of cultural life and of ideation"[2] and effects a secularization of consciousness as well: "An increasing number of individuals . . . look upon the world and their own lives without the benefit of religious interpretations."[3]

The approach to knowing that might be referred to as scientific objectivism resulted in a twofold loss which has had an immeasurable effect on modern spirituality. The commitment of science to affirming as real only what is discoverable and measurable with the senses, along with the reductive analyses of religious consciousness by Feuerbach, Nietzsche, Marx, and Freud combined to threaten the modern person's confidence in affirming transcendence. The modernist (scientistic) critiques of the notion of God made it impossible for many either to experience or to affirm on intellectual grounds a dimension of being or reality utterly surpassing our finite realm, which is a general way of describing transcendence. Transcendence as a "personal" God, of course, became for many especially untenable, both as concept and as experience.

But along with the loss of transcendence occasioned by the rise of modern science and the secularization it spawned was an equally significant loss, that of interior experience as a way of knowing the real. This might be designated as the loss of interiority. In its determination to purge the process of knowing from the distortions of passion and bias, modern science turned away from the inner experience of the knowing subject as a reliable or even significant element in the knowing process.

Now, ever since the late 1960s, in such fields as psychology, theology, sociology, the history of religions, and the philosophy of science, countless books have been published recounting the rise of modern science and its impact on our culture, demonstrating its epistemological shortcomings, its deleterious effect on our understanding of the individual and society, and its inadequacy for interpreting the questions of value, meaning, and other issues of ultimate concern.[4] Such has been the cumulative impact of these and other discussions and studies that it can now be said that intellectually we are in the postmodern era. The hegemony of modern science has been broken, in part by the very development of modern science itself, as in the areas of relativity theory and quantum mechanics.

But the society and culture at large are very pluralistic in regard to the reaction to the impact of modernity, and in our congregations themselves are to be found a variety of attitudes and orientations.

Some persons have simply been oblivious to modernity as far as its impact on their personal religious orientation is concerned. They have never accepted the implication that the authority of science should extend in any way to serve as an arbiter of what or how they should believe and practice their religion. Although they may be aware of some of the achievements of modern science and technology, in terms of their cognitive and religious existence these achievements have been given little attention. These persons continue to believe and practice what they understand as traditional religion in the way of their particular tradition.

There are others who affirm the same tradition in the same way but have been continually at war with modern science. They have not been oblivious; rather, they have been acutely aware of threats they see posed by modern science and mount vigorous attacks on the extension of modern science's claims and effects in the sphere of religion. They have sought to defend both Scripture and the beliefs of their traditions against attrition due to historical and scientific canons applied to Scripture and belief.

A third group would include those who have at one time felt themselves to be aligned with the processes of modernity, and have attempted to accommodate their religious beliefs and practices to the cognitive claims of modern science. For a variety of reasons these persons have become disillusioned with modernity. As Berger has pointed out in his book *The Heretical Imperative*,[5] Karl Barth's massive reaction against liberal theology as a result of the effect of World War I is an example of such disillusionment.

Within the past decade many pastors have found themselves disillusioned with modernity's promissory notes and now seek in the Christian historical tradition what they judge to be earlier and more reliable commentators on the nature and care of the soul. Thomas Oden's work[6] has found resonance in many pastors and lay persons who looked to psychology and sociology and the politics of social change for description and pursuit of religious meaning, and now feel that they have come up empty. For these persons, the rediscovery and reaffirmation of the tradition over against the hegemonistic cognitive and philosophical claims of modernity and its sciences are accompanied by a repudiation of earlier modernistic identifications. This response tends to obscure the degree to which the rediscovery was made possible by the very learning now repudiated.

This response is by no means limited to the intellectual leadership. Many laypersons have experienced a kind of mid-life modernity burnout. Without needing to advocate creationism as those in the first group might, and continuing to affirm historical-critical approaches to Scripture, these people nevertheless feel chastened intellectually and morally by what they feel was a too-ready acquiescence to ethical, philosophical, or behavioral propositions ranging from the replacement of koinonia groups by sensitivity groups, experimentation with hallucinogens, to the wholesale endorsement of welfare philosophies which are now identified with "modernity." The modernistic dalliance is now seen as deviance, and these persons now seek rerooting in the tradition.

Another group whose representatives are likely to be found in contemporary congregations are those who uncritically affirm all the critiques of modernity that have emanated from interpreters of archaic religion, the physics-mysticism analogizers, the perennial philosophists of modern mystic approaches, and the anti–mind-body separatists of holistic medicine.[7] These persons tend to experience the world-orientations presented in the various literatures as complementary to what they understand as the Christian tradition. A spirit of eclecticism characterizes these persons, who are less concerned about orthodoxy than about augmentation and expansion.

Rather than rerooting themselves in the tradition, these persons want to branch out into the leafy appeal of Eastern religions, new approaches to ecological living, and so on. These new directions are followed by some not so much in rejection or repudiation of science or modernity, as in the full enjoyment of these as foundational to their ventures. Questions of underlying compatibility between these movements and Christianity are not likely to occupy them. They continue their participation in congregations but follow these other pursuits as well.

But some among this group are self-consciously antimodernistic. They tend to see modern science as antagonistic to human values, mistrust medical intervention as mechanical intrusion, and advocate expansionist transpersonal psychology over against what they would see as humiliatingly reductionistic Freudian and post-Freudian depth psychology. They tend to affirm those aspects of the Christian tradition that apparently reinforce or echo their values, and ignore what does not.

A fifth position is distinct from all of the foregoing; it is what might be referred to as a postmodern stance. It seeks neither to refute, deny, nor repudiate the developments of modernity. It affirms several developments in recent intellectual history.

First, the separation of subject and object as the basis of knowing is now seen as appropriate only for a rather narrow range of investigation. Within the physical sciences themselves, subatomic physics has demonstrated that the observer very much influences what is observed, and that notions of specific cause and effect and simple location do not apply in the subatomic realm. Further, the fundamental principle of determinism has been undermined by the discovery that it is impossible to predict the behavior of subatomic particles apart from a "probability smear." This cluster of discoveries has challenged modern science's claims for certain knowledge of cause-effect relationships attained under conditions of untainted objectivity.

Second, modernity spawned what Paul Ricoeur has called the "hermeneutics of suspicion"[7] of Nietzsche, Marx, and Freud. These men, along with Feuerbach, unveiled projection as a fundamental element in religious ideation. Their reductionistic hermeneutics drove many in the church to attempt the articulation of religious ideas in the language of these various disciplines, accommodating to the relentless demands for a religion purged of desire, self-justification, and anthropomorphism. These men and their hermeneutics of suspicion unquestionably unmasked much self-deception in the religious consciousness, and we have not yet outrun their searchlights of analysis. Ricoeur has stated that "Freud changes consciousness by changing our knowledge of consciousness and by giving it the key to some of its deceptions."[8] Freud has decisively demonstrated that present in our religious symbolisms and behavior are derivatives of infantile instinctual and family conflict and the "strategies of desire" that are part of the substructure of the consciousness of all of us. We have not yet assimilated the full implications of this thrust of the Freudian analytic. Indeed, the following through of that analytic leads us to discover in ever new ways how the self-deceptions and strategies of desire weave themselves into the fabric of the very legitimations of our freedom from them.

This leads to the third element in this orientation, the quest for Being. If the "strategy of desire concealed in religious assertions"[9] is "the proper object of the analytic critique of religion,"[10] what it does not address is at once a more fundamental and comprehensive quest for the response to the whole of Being, experienced as "revealed to [the religious person] in a disposition to perceive a deeper reality under the appearance of objects and events . . . an overwhelming depth of being, a reality of such ontic richness that only the most comprehensive concepts approximate it."[11]

Such quest for and response to this depth always become expressed through (and are usually experienced in conjunction with) symbols and symbolic structures that do manifest the strategies of desire, but the religious phenomenon as a dimension of human being cannot be reduced to these strategies.

More will be presented concerning this dimension of religious experience. The purpose of presenting this here is to indicate a postmodern response to Freud as one of the prototypes of modern consciousness, a response that, rather than refuting Freud's modernist critique, seeks to include it in a more comprehensive understanding of the human informed by the full range of the disciplines of modernity rather than striking out from behind the walls of tradition. In this endeavor, modernity's disciplines both complement and relativize each other, so that the distinctiveness of the religious enterprise is enabled to stand out more clearly. This in turn permits an enriching of the complexity of the meanings of the religious symbolisms themselves, which faith then appropriates as graced.

A fourth element of the postmodern attitude is the determination to give prominence to experience. In a cultural situation of pluralism, differing religious and philosophical positions are seen to have legitimate claims to truth. Rather than simply perceive these in opposition to each other, it makes sense to understand that every formulation is a symbolic expression ultimately founded in experience, and to try to discern the nature of the experience so symbolized. Thus, for example, one whose view of the Christian life is essentially sacramental and one whose view is largely conversionistic need not relate to each other at the level of argument. One may proceed to learn what is the experience on which each position is based, and the meaning of that experience in the person's self-understanding. The one whose life is sustained by regular participation in the Holy Communion need not deny the legitimacy of the conversion/revival experience of the one who feels life to be sustained by the action of amazing grace in the recurrent experience of conversion.

A fifth element of postmodernity is the recovery of transcendence. At a fundamental level, the distinctiveness of the religious dimension of human experience is seen as the human experience of the transcendent (or what Berger calls the "supernatural"[12]), which is accompanied by the experience of what has been called the sacred or the holy. Such scholars as Berger and Robert Bellah, who are sociologists, and Mircea Eliade and Gerardus van der Leeuw, historians of religion, and Louis Dupre and Ricoeur, philosophers, have performed vital service to pastoral care and to contemporary ministry as a whole in facilitating clarity about this sui generis character of religion. This has been made possible only by the context of modernity, which has been able to bracket traditional claims of truth of religious systems and to look at them as they present themselves in human experience. In a broad sense, this is what the phenomenological approach intends. Berger has described phenomenology as "a method that investigates a phenomenon in terms of the manner in which it appears in human experience, without immediately raising the question of its ultimate status in reality."[13]

The implications of this carry in two directions. On the one hand, with a clearer idea of the religious dimension of human experience, we are more able to see that the modernist claims of doing away with religion are specious. Although, as Berger has wryly put it, "modern consciousness is not conducive to close contact with the gods,"[14] the religious response remains as a fundamental possibility. The sensitive pastor is able to discern and address this response as it idiosyncratically occurs among the people.

Another implication of this focus on "experience" of transcendence is that pastors may profitably devote a greater proportion of their energy to understanding the specifically religious dimension of parishioners' experience than has in recent decades been the tendency. It seems that pastors have either tended to see their role as inculcating a particular kind of religious experience or encouraging particular religious or ethical behavior; or, on the other hand, they have seen their role as strengthening the mental health of their people within the context of a religious institution with its overarching religious symbols.

All of these have their place in pastoral care. But for the specificity of the activity of the religious leader (which the pastor is), it might be more germane to understand the actual religious experience of the members of the congregation (and, to the extent possible, of the people of the community) and develop expertise in relating such experience to the various symbolic expressions of experience in the Christian tradition.

Pastors would want to know such information about their parishioners as When do they feel especially in touch with what is ultimately important to them? (or, in a more specifically religious formulation, When do they feel especially close to God?) or, Do they ever sense themselves as being very transient and dependent on a power that utterly surpasses human power? When do they feel most in touch with themselves, most who they are in the fullest way? What do they *experience* during worship (or, at Christmas, at Communion, etc.)?

For too long pastoral attention has been turned to the psychological or to the programmatic, or else there has been the assumption that the pastor has inherited custody of some normative formulation of experience which it is his or her responsibility to inculcate in the congregants. A more inductive attitude might lead down fruitful paths of pastoral nurture, not only in pastoral care but also in preaching and Christian education.

Finally, the foregoing suggests that pastoral care needs to recover the realm of interiority as it recovers the realm of transcendence. Again, interiority itself, under the influence of modernity, has tended to have been captured by depth psychology (when it wasn't declared nonexistent by behavioral psychology).

The recovery of interiority has three aspects to it. One is the development of the capacity to pay attention to one's own experience in its particularity and richness. This is not a call to mere subjectivity. As will be detailed later, this is a disciplined commitment of observation and attention, and is not an indulgence in mere feelings. It is a paying attention to what *is,* interiorly. This occurs both in one's action in the world, and in periods of reflection and recollection.

A second aspect is attention to interiority as one engages the symbols of the tradition. Again, the word "attention" is linked to interiority, and again, the aim is *not* the eliciting of any specific feelings. Rather, there is the submitting of oneself to engagement with the symbolic forms and acts of the tradition, and paying attention to what happens "within." This requires some discipline, and the appropriate observational attitude lends a kind of objectivity to the action.

A third aspect is the development of the capacity to be without interior images and feelings, to develop a capacity for interior emptiness. This is an ongoing dimension of prayer life, a rationale for which will be provided in a later chapter.

Such then are the elements of a postmodern perspective that aims to build on, incorporate, and delimit those aspects of modern thought most directly bearing on religion, rather than trying to ignore, refute, or repudiate them. It involves a recognition that the modern scientific enterprise has been relativized by its own post-Einsteinian developments on the one hand, and by the philosophical critiques on the other. These have demonstrated that an understanding of the human, and indeed the understanding of living animals, cannot be gained by studying them only according to methods developed for the study of inanimate objects. And especially when consciousness characterizes the subject of study, then the meaning of "objectivity" must be defined very carefully indeed. Objectivity appropriate to the study of human beings cannot be gained on the Cartesian principles of the separation of subject and object upon which modern science is based. Human experience does not lend itself to be understood when approached as analogous to the inert natural object.

It has been suggested in this chapter that this is especially so when the subject is human religious experience. Fundamental to this specific domain of human action has been the perception of the response to a realm of being transcendent to the given realm experienced in ordinary everyday consciousness. The positivist metaphysics underlying the scientism of modernity, of course, does not permit of this realm or realms. But the study of religion has demonstrated that one cannot understand human beings if one a priori excludes experience of this dimension from the realm of the possible and meaningful.

Religion is the human expression par excellence. Human beings symbolize their experience, and the symbols in turn channel and give meaning to experience. This dialectical relation of experience and symbolization is of the essence of human being, it is the matrix of meaning, and religions are the most profound, thoroughgoing, and comprehensive expression of that human essence.

Religions emerge from and carry forward the human experience of being in relation to the elements and dynamics of life and to the cosmos as a whole. In religion, the mode of knowing is not according to the Cartesian-scientistic model of the separation of subject and object; rather, it is a more intuitive mode in which one is impacted by particular meanings of life processes, historical events, or occurrences of nature; or one apprehends or experiences oneself as apprehended by a sense of depth in the midst of things, and in what sociologists and theologians have described as "limit-situations."

Of course, such experience never occurs in a vacuum of cultural and religious meanings, which are themselves conveyed through symbols. But each person's religious experience is to some extent unique since each person is to some extent unique. Thus each person experiences and attributes slightly different meanings to the symbols that both elicit and are used to express religious experience and meaning.

An example of how symbolization can function both to communicate and obscure meaning occurred when members of a seminary group (early adult to mid-forties) were discussing the importance of their experience of relationship to Jesus Christ. As each used the phrase others would nod understandingly. It was as if meaning were being communicated and shared. But upon inquiry none really knew what the content of the others' experience actually was. The phrase "relationship to Jesus" was specific to actual experience, but until they let go of the symbolization and talked about their experience, their actual experience was not known or understood by the others.

An approach to pastoral care informed by these perspectives is a more inductive approach, one that is attentive to a range of experience not confined to the neurotically conflicted, nor the response to crisis and trauma, nor even to the psychological dynamics of the developmental process. Rather, the pastor will help develop in the people a capacity for paying attention to those moments in which the structure of our ordinary every-day reality-oriented consciousness is modified by apprehensions of transcendence. These are moments (perhaps extended moments) marked by one or more of a diversity of qualities or characteristics. But the common element is the awareness that our ordinary everyday taken-for-granted reality is not the totality of reality.

Evelyn Underhill has written about the "parting of the conceptual veil" in moments of being in love, or listening to great music, or being caught up in the grandeur of a moment in nature or in the pathos of grief.[15] Of course, such moments might occur in conjunction with words or actions in a worship service. In these moments we experience what might be termed "truth in Being" different from empirical reality-truth.

Or they may be occasions such as Berger describes in *A Rumor of Angels:*[16] moments of reassurance, or humor, or moral outrage, when one's visceral conviction of the ultimate context of life breaks through in behavior that asserts the contingency, or transience, or aberrational quality of our created existence. Berger points to "prototypical human gestures"[17] which constitute "signals of transcendence"[18] pointing beyond the reality of our daily life. In this view, truth is not one thing. Truth lends itself to multiple modalities of manifestation. We become opened to what Paul Tillich called the dimensions of "depth" in a situation, or what Underhill called "a world . . . more valid . . . more rational . . . than that in which you usually dwell: a world which [has] a wholeness, a meaning, which exceed the sum of its parts."[19]

It is the case, then, that an enhanced quality of attention/ awareness may render many moments of so-called ordinary reality transparent to a different dimension of reality. The terminology at this point is purposely ambiguous because the specific quality of this awareness varies for different persons and at different times for the same person. Some would describe the awareness as of a different order of reality, or different realm. But others would be inclined to describe the experience as of reality as it really *is,* in its "isness," just *as such.* Still others would describe such experience as accompanied by a sense of "Presence," or a sense of "depth."

Throughout this discussion experience has been emphasized as a primary category (theology being reflection on experience), utilizing the symbolic structures of a given religion. But what also needs to be emphasized, and will be in later chapters, is the quality of attention through which we become aware of our experience. Experience becomes available to us according to the quality of our attention. Ignorance about the importance of attention is responsible for much of the superficial approach to prayer in the literature, and for the failure of many attempts by well-intentioned pastors and people to establish a mature and growing life of prayer. "Discipline" has typically been a word applied to scheduling and determination of will and other Protestant preoccupations.

The point is that the contemporary pastor ministers in a time and to a congregation in which some may adopt transcendence exclusively to very narrow conservative Protestant categories; others experience themselves as having lost all capacity for the experience of transcendence; others may be open to many varieties of transcendent experience but not be able to relate them coherently to the symbols of Christian faith. Amidst such diversity the pastor must recognize, point to, facilitate, and interpret moments of the experience of transcendence.

But the experiencing subject cannot be separated from the experienced object in the way neo-orthodox theology (especially that of Karl Barth) has suggested. Thus transcendence has also to be conceptualized as immanence. The One known as utterly surpassing all created beings is also known as permeating all structures and processes of life, even our knowing and experiencing itself. The great contemporary theologian and mystic Howard Thurman has called this the " 'givenness of God' . . . the movement of the heart of a man toward God; a movement that in a sense is within God—God in the heart sharing its life with God the Creator of all Life."[20] Thurman goes on to say, "It is not surprising that in man's spirit should be found the crucial nexus that connects him with the Creator of Life, the Spirit of the living God."[21]

Contemporary pastoral care needs to be informed by a way of thinking about spirit and Spirit that relates these terms to the contemporary psychology that undergirds most pastors' understanding of the person. Holistic pastoral care cannot operate on the basis of a bifurcated model of the human. In the next chapter we shall delineate the dimension of the human intended by the concept of spirit, and relate it to current psychological theories of the person. This task will lead us to an understanding of Spirit which will in turn shed light upon the possibility of the contemporary recovery of both transcendence and immanence.

CHAPTER 2

Spirituality
and Spirit

"Spirituality" is a term whose meaning is at once evident and elusive. It is a term of broad human scope, referring to many aspects of a person's or group's way of being. Because spirituality points to a reality of human being essential to religion, it is likewise essential that contemporary pastors have as clear an understanding as possible of what this concept refers to.

Our contemporary understanding of the person has been shaped by the influence of depth psychology. Many in the church have adapted a theological anthropology that is essentially depth psychology (Freudian or Jungian) baptized with Christian terms and concepts. On the other hand, a number of contemporary theologians (Reinhold Niebuhr, Will Herberg, Albert Outler and others) have examined Freudian theory and then sought to show psychology's inadequacy to account for the "higher" functions of human being. Currently there is a mood in some quarters to jettison the learning of depth psychology in favor of the insights into the human available in the Christian theological tradition.

But thinking about "spirit" must be continually informed by depth psychology, because depth psychology provides a thoroughgoing analysis of the way we become the kinds of persons we become and what keeps us that way. The kind of person we are deeply influences our spirituality; or more accurately, our spirituality is an expression of who we are.

At the same time, for specifiable reasons that are important to understand, depth psychology cannot provide us with a complete understanding of spirit. However, it is not immediately to theology but to the phenomenology of religion to which we must turn to augment the understanding of the human provided by depth psychology and the more recent psychology of consciousness. Phenomenology of religion is a very broad designation which includes sociological, anthropological, philosophical, and historical approaches to the understanding of religious phenomena. Phenomenologists attempt to describe human experience with the perspective(s) of their disciplines, without affirming or denying the claims to ultimate truth of the religious tradition being studied. They intend their language to be descriptive, whereas theological language emerges from a particular structure of faith, whose meanings and interpretations are embedded in its richly symbolic terminology.

The language of psychology and phenomenology can be more "experience-near" than theology usually is. By temporarily bracketing theological terms and concerns, we can look closely at the human phenomena. This movement, at first away from theological language toward more descriptive, experience-near language, enables a later recovery of theological language with a new specificity within its function of expressing a particular faith perspective. This chapter on spirituality and Spirit will illustrate this movement.

Sigmund Freud stands behind all contemporary depth psychology. We will understand our current situation better if we understand what he was about, and why "spirit" is not a category used by psychoanalysis. Freud was trained as a scientist, specializing in neurophysiology. He was committed to the scientific enterprise and to the career of being a scientist. He sought acceptance by the scientific community and (later) recognition of psychoanalysis as a science. For the first twenty years of his career, Freud was an eminently successful research scientist committed to the methodology of empirical investigations and verification.

Like other committed scientists, he saw science as a means of discovering truth free from the obscuring and inhibiting forces of passion and authority.[1] Since Francis Bacon the scientific method had promised a way to ascertain what is as it is, without the interference of emotional bias, wishful thinking, or the vested interests of those in temporal, intellectual, or ecclesiastical power. Freud thus shared certain basic post-Enlightenment assumptions about the nature, function, and promise of the scientific enterprise, and the progress that it would make possible.

After he stopped being a neurophysiologist and became a psychoanalyst he did not stop his commitment to the scientific approach. He regarded his clinical investigations as empirical research in which he discovered the data of human motivation, mental life, and behavior. As he was a scientist he attempted to construct a theory that could account for the startling data he was discovering.

As a psychoanalyst he was committed to ontogenetic explanation and interpretation of all behavior. That is to say, for Freud all behavior should be understood in terms of how it reflects the conflicts and resolutions of infancy and childhood, and these are—at root—instinctual.

In this regard Ludwig Binswanger—known for his contribution to existential psychoanalysis—reports a fascinating conversation with Freud. In the now-famous birthday conversation Freud said to his younger colleague, Binswanger, "Mankind has always known that it possesses spirit; I had to show it that there are also instincts."[2]

By "spirit" Freud apparently was referring to what are sometimes called the "higher" functions of the human—reason, intellect, the ethical capacity, conscience, and so on. He made the statement apparently because he so often was taken to task for emphasizing sex and aggressiveness as the essential human motives and capacities, and for seeing all of mental life, behavior, and culture as rooted in these "lower," "instinctual" drives. In the conversation with Binswanger Freud claimed that his theory of the human was in process and that persons misunderstood him when they assumed that he thought that his theory of instincts accounted for all human behavior and mental life. Binswanger, however, points out that "I have not found one place in all of Freud's monumental writings where he places 'the mind' or 'spirit' side by side with the instincts. . . . Everywhere in his writings human spirituality 'arises out of' instinctuality."[3]

All of the foregoing is reflected in Freud's analysis of religion. As is well known, Freud regarded religion as the illusory effort by humankind to overcome anxiety in the face of the uncontrollable forces of nature by personalizing them as gods; he also understood belief in a personal God (which is what Freud meant by religion) to be a projection of a wish for an all-powerful, benevolent, protective father. The religion of groups and individuals is characterized by the residue of the vicissitudes of the relationship with one's earthly parents. Freud was unquestionably a reductionist. Also, as a positivistic materialist he denied the existence of anything like a realm of reality transcendent to our empirical world. In addition, however much Freud admired intelligence, honesty, courage, and considerateness, and even self-consciousness, he did not turn his analytic attention to them except as they could be interpreted as reaction formation or sublimation, or some other defensive reaction.

But whereas Freud is often seen as the implacable and relentless opponent of much that we will consider in our study of spirituality, his discoveries and those of his followers are exceedingly useful in helping us to understand many of the puzzling human dynamics of spirituality, even if they are not able to account for "spirit" itself.

I have devoted so much consideration to Freud because his discoveries and analysis have so heavily influenced our contemporary culture and the methods and—too often—the assumptions of pastoral care. In order to recover and affirm our vocation, we must wrest it from the grip of strictly Freudian assumptions about the human. But to be significantly engaged with the profound human struggles we must integrate and build on much of what Freud and his followers have to teach us.

Freud saw very clearly how theological concepts and affirmations can foreclose exploration of the connection between adult and childhood experience and behavior. Pastors should not be guided by Freud's rejection of theology and religious experience but by the principle that the more we can understand how persons' life experiences influence and are expressed through their religious formulations, the more profoundly we will be able to understand and minister to them.

As is well known, Freud presented a massive challenge to theology. Neo-orthodox Protestant theologians tended to respond to Freud by "granting him the low ground." Freud's analysis of the human (their arguments tended to run) demonstrated how persons are and get to be neurotic or sick, and thus they also might apply to neurotic or sick religion. But a theological understanding of the actions of God's grace is necessary, they maintained, in order to account for the capacity of humans to overcome the conflicts of their nature as described by Freud.

Prior to the mid-1920s, Freud's attention had focused on the unconscious causes of psychological conflict. Then in this period he began to turn his attention to the question of how the person is able to function in spite of the enormous tensions between the demands of external "reality," the instinctual demands, and the demands of what he later referred to as the superego. Out of this interest evolved his structural theory of the personality, the theory of id, ego, and superego.

But Freud never gave up his notion that all behavior is rooted in unconscious instinctual conflict, the needs of sexuality, aggression, and protection.

The development of psychoanalytic theory by no means terminated with Freud. Expansion and revision of the theory has continued, on the basis of further clinical investigation in psychotherapy and extensive study of children, parents, and families. This work has broadened and deepened the understanding of early mother-child interactions and their influence on later personality trends and characteristics, and their influence on religious beliefs and attitudes. Ego psychology and object relations theory are the two major contemporary developments of Freud's psychoanalytic theory.

Therapists, researchers, and theoreticians understand themselves within a scientific context. This means that in their analysis and theorizing they maintain an empiricist, positivistic approach.

Freud himself led the redirection of attention from unconscious instinctual process to the processes by which the ego compromises and synthesizes the "demands" of id, superego, external reality, and self-preservation. This marked the beginnings of a shift from the question, What are the unconscious causes of disturbance? to, How does the ego function to enable a person to cope? Erik Erikson eventually took the question one step further, asking, in effect, How do we recognize and account for healthy personality development? Erikson sees personality development as a lifelong process of the formation and maintenance of ego-identity, formed, threatened, and reformed through eight stages, each with its characteristic threats and opportunities, each marked by its own psycho-sexual-social dynamics and challenges. Each stage is marked by the focal emergence of a basic human need and capacity—trust, autonomy, initiative, industry, identity, intimacy, generativity, and wisdom.

Erikson developed an approach to instinct that moves away from the model of quanta of energy to describe basic human drives and needs in terms of experienceable capacities which develop with the psychosocial matrix. Fundamental human motivation, "instinctual" needs and behaviors, range, in Erikson's theory, from hunger and sex to ideology (structure of meaning) and to interpersonal intimacy and care. The central image in his theory is that of ego-identity, the inner sense of self-continuity through time in a social context in which one's identity is confirmed by valued others.

Of course, identity can be stronger or weaker, more or less cohesive, more or less rigid, more or less able to relate to others, more or less adaptable to change. Erikson wanted to discover and to prescribe what kinds of experience are essential to develop and maintain "healthy" identity. As a theoretician of the person, Erikson has been free from several nineteenth-century intellectual assumptions that inhibited Freud's theorizing about the person. (1) Freud was influenced by a basically mechanistic image in terms of which he sought to explain human motivation and behavior according to force and energy in a closed system. (2) Freud was committed to an epistemology of naive realism that assumed a neat separation of subject and object. (3) Freud was a strict cause-effect determinist who believed that a phenomenon had to be explained in terms of its antecedent cause, and once this was found the meaning of the phenomenon was reduced to the antecedent.

From the time of his first major book, *Childhood and Society,* Erikson has maintained that the human being cannot be understood within a theory founded on these presuppositions. In the first pages of this book he denies the adequacy of the "specific location" (discrete cause and effect) theory of neurotic disturbance; he recognizes the inevitable influence of the psychoanalytic observer on that which he is observing, and thereby moves from a subject-object epistemology to a recognition that the act of knowing in a person is ultimately a transaction between knower and known; he recognized that the mind-body dualism or mind-body-others triplicity is an artificial abstraction; and he stated that emotional disturbance has to do not so much with merely the conflict of libido and aggression as with a disturbance of the central ordered and "ordering core" of the person.[4]

Erikson has always sought to sustain the location of his theory and therapy within the psychoanalytic tradition, even though—as pointed out above—he viewed certain meta-theoretical assumptions as being invalid for an understanding of the human. But if he emphasized that personality development is a lifelong process, he also retained the psychoanalytic view of the importance of childhood. And if he did not share Freud's view of the exhaustive significance of sexuality and aggression, he did assert that every stage in human development carries with it legacies from the earlier stages, and every conflict has a somatic dimension which we ignore at great risk to full understanding of the person. And if he acknowledged that strong identity requires coherent ideology and social engagement (the quest for meaning), he also detailed how the "solution" will reflect the fundamental psycho-sexual-social problematics and strengths that have characterized the person's history since infancy.

So it is that Erikson has sought, within the parameters of psychoanalytic thinking (which he helped to expand), ways to account for what religionists and humanists alike have often pointed to as the spiritual dimension in the human, or, simply, the spirit.

In so doing Erikson demonstrated that psychology could indeed include within its anthropology those higher functions of the human that theological critics of Freud claimed psychology did not deal with and which they designated as "spirit." Purpose, meaning, self-transcendence—these were held to be God-given, not rooted in the dynamics of instincts and early infantile conflict. Erikson has been instrumental in providing an anthropology that helps us overcome such artificial distortions as higher-lower, body-mind, physical-mental, and instinctual-spiritual.

While Erikson and others were working within the psychoanalytic tradition, from within academic psychology and counseling Carl Rogers and Abraham Maslow were developing, on the basis of their observation and research, a theory of the person that maintained that there is a fundamental human drive or need for what they called "self-actualization." The "self" (a theoretical construct that Freud did not postulate) has needs for the enhancement of experience, for stimulation, for complexity. Maslow wrote of a "hierarchy of needs" and maintained that when needs such as those for food, shelter, and basic security of person were met, then the human (and specifically human) needs for enhancement of being came focally into play.

For our purposes it is not necessary to go into detail in exposition of their theories. The point of view they articulate and support is represented by Hadley Cantril, who in sophisticated cross-cultural research (informed by his work in the perspective of Rogers, Maslow, and other "humanistic" psychologists) found common "functional uniformities" that he claimed were at least in part attributable to a "genetically built-in design."[5] These include survival needs for food, shelter, security; a need for order; the need to enlarge satisfaction (similar to Robert White's notions of play and competence[6] and other theories of adience-motivation); hope in the future (in part related to confidence in the society of which the person is a member), and capacity and opportunity to make choices; the needs for identity and a sense of worthwhileness and self-esteem; and the need for a system of values.[7]

In addition to the humanistic approach in psychology, there was also Existential psychology represented by Rollo May, Victor Frankl, and others, who maintained that it is impossible to understand the human being as human unless one takes account of the human need to experience meaning and purpose. In the sustained absence of the experience of meaning and purpose, human being degenerates into neurosis and despair.

The reason for briefly reminding the reader of these developments in post-Freudian psychology is to point out that contemporary psychology has no difficulty accounting for those elements of human being that theologians claimed were not derived from the vicissitudes of the "instinctual" nature of the human. While the theologians were contending against Freud, they thought they were demonstrating the need for a theory of grace, spirit, or image of God as something other than the instinctual, psychological, genetic equipment of the human. But the humanistic and ego psychologists showed that concepts of will, freedom, meaning, self-transcendence, and sacrifice do not require a theory of the infusion of "spirit" in order to "explain" the human.

It is not the case that the concept "spirit" has pointed us to an illusory dimension of the human. But as it had come to us in theology it perpetuated a dichotomous doctrine of the human which was not adequate to account for the data regarding illness, healing, and health generated by the psychoanalytic movement. In the light of what we now know about the importance of childhood psychosocial experience for adult personhood, theological anthropologies that try to explain behavior merely in terms of the adult will and rationality are simply begging the question.

Therefore, a useful contemporary approach to spirit and

spirituality must understand these terms and clarify them in ways congruent with the best psychological anthropology. In order to clarify its own concepts and to establish itself as a significant discipline of inquiry, psychoanalysis had to distance itself from such concepts as "spirit."

This was because, as employed in Christian theology and in the European intellectual milieu of the rise of psychoanalysis, "spirit" functioned precisely in opposition to "nature." The possibility of an ontogeny of "spirit" was thereby precluded by the assumptions about the human dominant in the nineteenth century (and traceable back to Augustine of Hippo and his use of Platonic anthropology).

What Erikson, White, and the humanistic and Existential psychologists have accomplished is a more unified model of the person, a model that helps us move beyond the one inherited from the theological tradition that in effect describes adult humans (implicitly male) as discontinuous with their childhood history, functioning with a will and intellect related to the body and the person's history of relationships only in terms of opposition.

In addition to the psychoanalytic and humanistic psychologies that have expanded their theories in such a way that accommodates much of what religionists and theologians mean by "spirit," the transpersonal approach in psychology has developed into a movement that includes persons studying altered states of consciousness, the effects of psychotropic drugs, meditation, biofeedback, Eastern religions, and so on. The scope of interest of this group is suggested by a selection from the first issue of the *Journal of Transpersonal Psychology*.

Transpersonal Psychology is the title given to an emerging force in the psychology field by a group of psychologists and professional men and women from other fields who are interested in those *ultimate* human capacities and potentialities that have no systematic place in positivistic or behavioristic theory ("first force"), classical psychoanalytic theory ("second

force"), or humanistic psychology ("third force"). The emerg
ing Transpersonal Psychology ("fourth force") is concerned
specifically with the *empirical,* scientific study of, and responsible
implementation of the findings relevant to, becoming, individual
and species-wide meta-needs, ultimate values, unitive consciousness, peak experiences, B. values, ecstasy, mystical experience,
awe, being, self-actualization, essence, bliss, wonder, ultimate
meaning, transcendence of the self, spirit, oneness, cosmic
awareness, individual and species-wide synergy, maximal interpersonal encounter, sacralization of everyday life, transcen-
dental phenomena, cosmic selfhumor and playfulness, maximal sensory awareness, responsiveness and expression, and
related concepts, experiences, and activities. As a definition,
this formulation is to be understood as subject to *optional* individual or group interpretations, either wholly or in part, with
regard to the acceptance of its content as essentially naturalistic,
theistic, supernaturalistic, or any other designated classifica-
tion.[8]

Transpersonal psychologists and psychologists of consciousness claim William James, not Freud, as their founding
father, and are led by James's famous statement: "Our normal
waking consciousness, rational consciousness as we call it, is but
one special type of consciousness, whilst all about it, parted
from it by the filmiest of screens, there lie potential forms of
consciousness entirely different."[9] As the definition of reality
assumed by modern science is a function of our ordinary,
everyday rational consciousness, so there may be alternate
realities discoverable in altered states of consciousness.

Transpersonal psychology is not interested in verifying
truth claims of various types of religious experience. Rather, it
regards religious experience (including mystical experience)
as part of being human and as a manifestation of human
potentialities of being which psychology is specially qualified to
investigate. Its interest in psychological investigation has not
as yet been matched by sophistication in the inevitable philosophical issues inherent in the study of comparative religion, nor in contemporary developments in hermeneutics,

which examine the relationship between tradition, text, and experience.

Charles Tart, one of the leading proponents and theoreticians of transpersonal psychology, has chosen to use the word "spiritual" to apply to "that vast realm of human potential dealing with ultimate purposes, with higher entities, with God, with life, with compassion, with purpose."[10] Such a broad designation is reminiscent of the theologian John Macquarrie's ultimately tautological description of "spirit": "A capacity for going out of oneself and beyond oneself . . . for transcending oneself, . . . freedom, creativity, this capacity for going beyond any given state in which he finds himself, that makes possible self-consciousness and self-criticism, understanding, responsibility, the pursuit of knowledge, the sense of beauty, the quest of the good, the formation of community, the outreach of love and whatever else belongs to the amazing richness of what we call the 'life of the spirit.'"[11]

We see here a problem that exists in both psychology and theology in regard to the understanding and description of "spirit." It is used to refer to such a wide variety of human behavior and experience that it loses specificity. It becomes a cover word to refer to "higher" functions of the human, and by employing the word "spirit" seems to close them off from possible influence by any of the so-called "lower" functions of the human.

Such non-specific use of the term seems, unfortunately, inevitable; and this work will not be able to avoid these difficulties. It is simply the case that "spirit" has in fact been broadly used, but we must try to bring into focus the meanings we will attach to it. There will inevitably be some arbitrariness about this delimitation, but I think we can introduce some coherence and consistency in our usage.

With the emergence of this interest within the psychological "establishment," research, therapeutic, and experiential interests are being turned to much of what has in the past been regarded as the domain of institutionalized religious experience. This approach attempts to study with empiricism appropriate to the subject matter much that in conventional religious language would be designated as mystical, spiritual, revelatory, and/or transcendent experience. Transpersonal psychologists assume that consciousness is not reducible to the conflicts of sexuality, aggression, and self-preservation. Rather, transpersonal psychology holds open for investigation the legitimacy of the claims of experience that involve transpersonal phenomena. Transpersonal experience is experience that is restricted to neither intrapersonal nor interpersonal dynamics. It may include these dynamics but it cannot be fully accounted for in terms of them. The interests of this group tend to be in phenomena of consciousness, which it regards as the proper arena of psychological inquiry.[12]

The significance of transpersonal psychology is that it does not limit its understanding of "reality" either to the naive realism of Freud and the behaviorists, nor to the somewhat more sophisticated view of ego psychologists and object relations theoreticians. These latter describe human behavior and experience in our ordinary, everyday, basic state of consciousness. They study religious experience as it reflects childhood and adult developmental vicissitudes.

SPIRIT IN THE
HEBREW AND GREEK TRADITIONS

In the Western tradition, "spirit" is etymologically related, in both Hebrew *(ruach)* and Greek *(pneuma)*, to the concepts of breath and wind. In Hebrew anthropology, *ruach* was the enlivening force of a person: when the breath went out of a person, the life went out. The Hebrew model of the human was different from the prevailing contemporary view of the person as encapsulated within the confines of the skin.

In the Yahwist creation story, Yahweh breathed his breath into the rolled dust, and with the breath the dust became a living *nephesh*. Thus the very being of the person is permeated by the *ruach*, the breath of God. It was the *ruach* of God that hovered over the waters of chaos in the Priestly creation story. The point for our purposes is that the human capacity for participation in and responsiveness to the essential dynamism of the transcendent is represented in the Hebrew concept of *ruach*-spirit. The enlivening principle of the human is one with the enlivening principle of the divine, in relation to which the human is utterly contingent.

In Greek the situation becomes more complex, because although initially *pneuma* referred to wind, breath, energy, dynamic reality, "spirit" came to be juxtaposed to the body and to matter. This is alien to biblical anthropology on the whole. Paul has some traces of this in his writing, as does the Johannine literature, but the situation is highly ambiguous. When Paul juxtaposes *pneuma* and *sarx*, he is juxtaposing not substances but tendencies and potentialities of an indivisible unity of the human. It is in the gnostic developments of Platonism that we see most fully developed the split of spirit and body. Thus "spirit" came to be identified with the realm of the eternal, the real, the ideal; there was a dichotomy of spirit and body, in which the body was understood as corruptible and corrupting, the spirit as pure in itself. But still, there is retained in the Greek concept the notion of a dimension of the human that is capable of participation in and (in Greek Neoplatonic mysticism) union with the divine.

Both the Hebrew and the Greek concepts are fundamentally opposed to the modern, scientific view of the human which ignores the dimension of transcendence in any form and views the person as entirely a "natural" phenomenon—natural in this case meaning of nature, which is ultimately material and explainable in terms of mechanical physiochemical processes.

Some of the ambiguity regarding the reference of the word "spirit" occurs because it is used to refer to two very different facets of the person. On the one hand, "spirit" is used to refer to the human capacity for response to the lure of the good, the appreciation and creation of beauty, the ability to persevere in adversity, the capacity to exercise free choice. In terms of ego psychology, these are indications of the strong, integrated, and integrating ego, one of the marks of which is, according to Erik Erikson, the capacity to make choices and to make them stick. Thus loosely used, "spirit" refers to those "higher" or stronger capabilities of the human. These capacities manifest themselves as signs of strength in the person who has derived from the life cycle identity and integrity within a structure of meaning (which includes "ideology" in Erikson's terminology).

Since Freud's theory of the origins of neurosis could not (and was not intended to) account for "health," theologians seized on the indisputable presence of these qualities as evidence of something that went beyond the psychosexual givens of "natural man" as described by Freud. Thus the categories of "image of God" and "spirit" were invoked to account for these "self-transcending" capabilities and to demonstrate that Freud's biopsychological anthropology requires theological correction. In a curious way, these theologians continued a Hellenistic principle of the separation of spirit and body, or nature.

SPIRIT AS RESPONSIVENESS TO TRANSCENDENT MEANING

There is another understanding of "spirit" that does not fall into the trap of the God-of-the-gaps response of the theologians, nor is it synonymous with those aspects of personality designated as ego-strengths and capacities. This view of spirit points to that evolved quality of awareness, that capacity or aspect of our personhood that is able to respond to our human experience of birth, death, suffering, joy, sex, beauty, nature, and tragedy, as reflective of and participative in power and meaning that transcend our created (given) life and upon which our life is experienced as being contingent.

Phenomenologists of religion have demonstrated that this human perception occurs in all human groups, of whatever ethnographical grouping. It is not the case that the religious symbol systems that articulate this fundamental awareness are in fact reducible to the economic arrangements of the tribe, or the family structures, or early infantile experience. None of these can be held to be "prior" to religious awareness and systems any more than they are prior to the language of a tribe. Both religion and language are coemergent with the human.

It *is* the case that economics, kinship, infantile experience, sexual attitudes, hunting or agricultural priorities, and so on, are expressed in religion. Religion functions to integrate, to bind the whole of significant human experience into structures of meaning, what Erikson has called ideology. But permeating all the systems is the experience of our given life as impacted by, reflective of, and contingent upon a dimension of reality transcendent to that of ordinary day-in and day-out reality.

This quality of awareness and response is not derived from "more basic" human instincts, as Freud would have it. It is a capacity sui generis with being human. The response of the human to what Mircea Eliade has called the Sacred, or Gerardus van der Leeuw has called "mana" (power), and Tillich has called the "actualization of power and meaning in unity," an order of reality prior to and greater than our own, is coemergent with human being. There are no logical or philosophical arguments that can demonstrate that such response is reducible to the conflicts and needs of infancy. In different cultures and different periods this fundamental capacity is symbolized and manifested differently. Religions are not "all the same," but they emerge from this same human capacity to experience life in relationship to a perceived dimension of power and meaning experienced as transcendent to our own.

The question naturally arises, Is this simply a human projection, or does the human response-capacity respond to something that is "real" or "out there"?

Scientific materialism's assertion that the physical world is the "real" world rests on unsustainable epistemological assumptions. In an extended and detailed analysis, Daniel Yankelovitch and William Barrett have persuasively analyzed those assumptions and have delineated the fundamentals of a twentieth-century philosophical consensus that affirms an alternative to scientific materialism more appropriate to understanding human experience and the question of the really real.

In brief, Yankelovitch and Barrett maintain that one "cannot begin an explanation of human experience by saying that some parts of our experience are not really real, but merely an appearance or screen for what is really real."[13] Those psychological or philosophical or philological approaches that assert that religious experience of the holy or of transcendence can only be illusory or delusional base their assertion on untenable pre-Kantian, materialist philosophical assumptions that limit reality to "aspects of matter."[14] After a comprehensive analytical argument, Yankelovitch and Barrett assert that "the really real is located in the raw experiential world of the individual, to be comprehended without a priori judgment as to what is primary or secondary, truth or delusion."[15]

Of course, the response to transcendence is always mediated through specific cultural forms (usually, but by no means always) within a given religious symbol system. Also, the response is a part of a given personality structure, and although it may reflect that structure it is not reducible to the early infantile experience that underlies the personality. Now this is complicated, because personality factors can in fact so constrict this capacity that it does little more than reflect the basic personality conflicts, so that Freud's accusation of projection in some cases holds. Every serious religious tradition has had to wrestle with this problem of the differentiation of response from projection. In the Christian tradition this is known as the problem of discernment.

And, indeed, we can now see how this reality is central to ministry. "Spirit" in this sense points to the human capacity to experience and respond to the events of one's life and times as reflective of a reality transcendent to our own. In the Christian tradition, God, Christ, Jesus, Holy Spirit, and the cross are symbols that both point to this reality and express it. "Growth in grace," or "spiritual nurture," is the process of deepening and strengthening persons' responsiveness (in terms of awareness, understanding, and behavior) to the reality made manifest by these symbols. We are describing here a process in which both consciousness and behavior are strengthened, and thereby reinforce each other. Nurturing and guiding this process will be discussed in detail in chapter 4.

We have seen that "spirit" has been used to refer to those "higher" human capacities, once claimed by theology, now accounted for within psychology. It is also—and more properly and specifically—used to designate the human capacity to perceive and respond to a dimension of reality transcendent to our ordinary, everyday reality.

SPIRIT AS THE CAPACITY FOR UNION

A third referent of "spirit" has to do with a different sort of phenomenon from what we have been discussing. Spirit as we have just been describing it is a function, capacity, aspect, or dimension of the human personality as it develops throughout the life cycle within a specific community during a particular historical period. As such it is intertwined with and expressive of our particular experienced personality and character. The third referent of spirit to which we now turn is also held to be a constant of the human. It is that in the human which longs for union with the whole of Being. Depth psychologists and Protestant theologians alike have tended either to ignore, deny, or distort this aspect of the human.

Freud, for example, simply denied that anything like the "oceanic feeling"[16] had independent status within personality structure or motivation. He accounted for it as "another way of disclaiming the danger which the ego recognizes as threatening it from the external world."[17]

Protestant theologians have tended to regard this aspect of spirit as a theological distortion. One might have *communion* with God, but no union. Communion is an encounter between self and self. "Union" suggests the possibility of the identity of the human and the divine. But there is an infinite qualitative difference, these theologians would maintain, between God and the human, and there is nothing in the human ontologically that can unite with God. The human is utterly dependent on the self-initiated active grace of God engaging us. We in turn have only the capacity to respond, and that itself is interpreted as the action of grace in us; or, as some would express it, the *imago Dei* is that which enables us to respond to the unmerited active grace of God.

But even if the theologians eschew the notion of "union" they still recognize the human yearning for the divine. One frequently encounters in their writings the words of Augustine: "O God, Thou hast made us for thyself, and our hearts are restless until they find their rest in thee." This is an expression of the basic human need to experience participation in a source of power and meaning that is of greater magnitude than our own. Ethnography and the history of religions demonstrate that this has been part of the human behavior and response repertoire as far back as there have been human beings. The evidence seems to suggest that in earlier epochs the experience tended to be more a sense of participation in a world that was suffused with power and meaning rather than either union with it or relationship "over against it." And yet the experience of relationship in some way has always been a part of this dimension.

But both Freud and the theologians give priority to their assumptions regarding what is genuine and legitimate rather than give credence to the reports of serious mystics and others whose experience does not accord with their frameworks. Here is an example of how both interpretive psychology and theology can benefit from a phenomenological perspective. In both cases fundamental epistemological and ontological issues are at stake as well as questions of anthropology. Both Freud and the theologians identify the person with the personality as it develops within the family and the widening psychosocial radius.

Basically, this is the critique of contemporary psychology articulated by the transpersonal psychologists. Those who study the effect of drugs, meditation, hypnosis, and mystical experience are realizing that an essential element of human being is the perception of our participation in structures of power and meaning that transcend our ordinary state of consciousness, our personality as formed in the matrix of family and social experience. These structures of power and meaning are knowable by means that may include but also transcend ordinary sense experience and its technological extensions. In this third designation of "spirit" it is maintained that spirit is that by which we experience our oneness with the ultimate.

Although they articulate it in many different ways, mystics maintain that union with the ultimate only occurs when the attachments by which we establish, experience, and sustain our identity are dissolved. In this perspective, personality and identity are impediments to the realization of union. With their investment in projects of all kinds, their mechanism of defense, their need for confirmation, their attachment to "creatures" (as the anonymous author of *The Cloud of Unknowing* calls all created finite things, feelings, and ideas that deflect attention from God), personality and identity absorb our energy and attention, and we lose access to what many have held to be the ultimately real and enduring dimension of our being.

Experiences of union happen to one; they are not to be achieved. Serious spiritual disciplines aim at a continual clearing away of the impediments to unitive experience; they do not claim to bring it about. As Gerald May has pointed out, any self-definitional activity militates against unitive experience.[18]

Therefore, those psychologies that focus on the contents of consciousness—images, feelings, memories, thoughts, ideas—tend to ignore or deny that dimension of human being which is most able to "inform" and assure us of our ultimately unalienated status in the cosmos. That is why adequate anthropologies—theories of the human—must pay attention to the serious mystics. They report to us observations and learnings about human experience every bit as demonstrable as and philosophically more important than what is observable in psychotherapy. This is by no means to denigrate the significance of the discoveries of Freud and his followers. But their work was carried out without reference to or in denial of this crucial dimension of human experience.

Carl Gustav Jung is something of an exception among psychologists. He was sensitive to what he regarded as religious experience. However, his definitions of religion as the "careful and scrupulous observation of . . . the numinosum"[19] and his understanding of how this observation is carried out are entirely dependent upon the self-defining images that emerge from the unconscious. While this process certainly has a role in religious experience, Jung was thoroughly skeptical of and warned against Westerners exploring realms of consciousness devoid of images. This, combined with Jung's reduction of all religious imagery to the categories of his own psychology, render him an unreliable guide for Christian spirituality. This is not to deny Jung's brilliance nor his enormously significant contribution to our understanding of symbolic and healing processes of the psyche. But these two reservations account for why Jung's work is not much referred to in this book.

Now, to return to the main line of our argument: One major referent of spirit is that dimension of the person capable of unitive experience, which underlies the personality or character structure and does not require perceptions, images, thoughts, or feelings as vehicles for our awareness of it.

In this context, "spirit" is close to the meaning of "heart" in the anthropology of Greek and Russian Orthodox Christianity. "Heart" refers to the center of the person where, as Timothy Ware expresses it, he or she discovers "first the god-like spirit which the Holy Trinity implanted in man at creation, and with this spirit . . . comes to know the Spirit of God."[20] Thomas Merton says that "' the heart' . . . refers to the deepest psychological ground of one's personality, the inner sanctuary where self-awareness goes beyond analytical reflections and opens out into metaphysical and theological confrontation with the Abyss of the unknown yet present—one who is more 'intimate to us than we are to ourselves.' "[21]

"Heart" and "spirit" are transpersonal concepts; they suggest a dimension of human being in ontological continuity—even identity—with God. In Greek and Russian Orthodoxy heart and spirit are often described as including emotions, will, and conscience, just as Protestant theologians often employed "spirit" to designate those. But in addition, for the Eastern Orthodox, "heart" and "spirit" affirm the principle of unity with God, a unity that can be known only through deep prayer. The disciplines of mysticism were developed in order to enable the clearing away or the falling away of the impediments to the realization of the essential unity of the human with the divine.

SPIRITUALITY

In the light of the complex history of the term, it is appropriate to try to be more specific about what we shall mean by "spirituality." Fortunately, several recent authors have provided definitions that point to particular aspects of "spirituality" in continuity with the way in which we have understood spirit.

Paul Tillich has already provided us with our most inclusive definition of "spirit," namely, "the actualization of power and meaning in unity." This definition opens for us the immense reach of "spirit" and enables us to perceive the continuity between disparate areas of experience as manifestations of this essential human capacity. We should keep this definition of Tillich's in conjunction with his definitions of a symbol. Power and meaning become actualized through symbols which themselves participate in the specific power and meaning.

Drawing on Tillich's terms, then, spirituality would refer to the way one keeps oneself receptive and responsive to the actualization of power and meaning in unity. One's spirituality would be reflected and expressed in the particular symbols one was drawn to and utilized in one's religious expression and self-understanding.

In his posthumously published book, *Spirituality for Ministry,* Urban T. Holmes presents a five-point definition of spirituality as "(1) a human capacity for relationship (2) with that which transcends sense phenomena; this relationship (3) is perceived by the subject as an expanded or heightened consciousness independent of the subject's efforts, (4) gives substance in the historical setting, and (5) exhibits itself in creative actions in the world."[22]

Holmes touches on the essential points of spirituality while leaving unspecified the content of such terms as "relationship," "transcendent," and "heightened consciousness." This definition compresses much of what we have been discussing up to now. Spirituality is the specifically human capacity to experience, be conscious of, and relate to a dimension of power and meaning transcendent to the world of sensory reality expressed in the particularities of a given historical and social context, and leads toward action congruent with its meaning. Obviously, many different religious orientations can be accommodated by this definition, and even diverse Christian orientations.

John Eusden and John Westerhoff have described spirituality this way:

> At the center of all human life is the quest for the integration of the material and the nonmaterial, the body and the soul, the secular and the sacred. Spirituality has to do with being an integrated person in the fullest sense. We humans seem to know that we are more than physical bodies and intellects, that our environment is more than the physical universe known only indirectly through sense experience, and reason. We seem to grasp that we are also comprised of a nonphysical dimension which can be known directly by encounter and participation.[23]

They emphasize integration in their concept of spirituality. The metaphor "integration" is significant since it suggests the progressive coherence of broader and deeper ranges of experience and reality in the being and identity of the person. Thus "becoming" might be substituted for "being" in the phrase "being an integrated person." Spirituality is a dynamic reality; thus there is no endpoint, no moment when one has "arrived" spiritually. The mystery of spirit becomes ever more complex.

Gerald May is another contemporary writer who has attempted to express the meaning of spirituality. In his important recent book, *Will and Spirit,* May says, "Spirituality consists of an experienced and interpreted relationship among human beings and the mystery of creation."[24]

It is worth noting that affective experience and the cognitive and the social are all given prominence by May in this very concise definition. He does not limit spirituality to the realm of feelings, nor does he support a privatized image of spirituality. Rather, this statement reminds us that we are embodied, affectual, social, and "minded" beings, and that all of these dimensions participate in our relation to the mystery of creation.

Within all of these descriptions of spirituality runs the affirmation of the essential continuity of the human with the transcendent (Holmes), the sacred (Eusden and Westerhoff), and the mystery of creation (May). And all of these writers recognize that there are in human experience moments of heightened awareness of the continuity, sometimes to the point of an experience of union, in which one's own self-defining activities attenuate or cease.[25] These unitive experiences, as May and others call them, vary in intensity or depth and in the degree to which they are interpreted and reflected on with theological symbols. It is clear that while these experiences are of great significance, they are not the aim or purpose or goal of spirituality. They are graced events that occur in many different contexts and cannot be forced by so-called spiritual disciplines.

At the same time, however, since our culture's norms, values, and epistemological assumptions militate against the kind of awareness of the ultimate nature and context of our lives toward which the concept of spirituality points, the importance of habits and practices conducive toward and expressive of this awareness is obvious.

Spirituality cannot be limited to the sphere of the discipline of mysticism aimed at unitive experience. This is a false image of spirituality. But those who respond to the lure of deeper relationship with or awareness of the transcendent, sacred mystery of creation discover that some actions enrich while others inhibit that response. Therefore, this book will give substantial attention to those private and corporate disciplines that Christians (and others) through the centuries have found conducive to relationship with the response to the tremendous mystery of God.

But these disciplines selected will all share one fundamental quality: they carry the person into, not away from, lived experience. So much is this the case that awareness of transcendence may in fact be indistinguishable from the awareness of immanence. With this statement the bias of this book is made clear: lived experience is the center of spirituality. Disciplines of prayer, worship, and engagement with the world are vehicles for the awareness of God present in, permeating, emerging from our lived experience.

This requires an image of God different from the objectified, distant, exclusively transcendent being which is the image of much Protestant and Catholic spirituality. Locating spirituality within lived experience may seem tautological if not specious. After all, what is not, finally, lived experience? The point is that spirituality is not to be identified with correct thinking, nor with only certain feelings, nor with holding the right beliefs, nor even with certain kinds of action in the world, even though spirituality frequently does become so identified.

Rather, spirituality has to do with how all these spheres of life, including our relationships, are integrated in our awareness. Spirituality is a "holistic, functional orientation to being"[26] which reflects our relationship to that which in its infinite capacity for immanence is known as utterly transcendent, and whose transcendence, by our very capacity to experience it, is known as also immanent.

In spirituality, mind and body, intellect and feeling, belief and action are not understood as being necessarily in opposition. Rather, they are complementary modes of experiencing and responding to what is. The expansion of our awareness and the integration of our experience occurs in conjunction with an ongoing encounter with sacred Scripture and the tradition. For example, as women have become critically self-aware of their historical experience within the structures of Christian theology and institutions, they have discovered that there are ways of experiencing, articulating, and participating that differ from what has been the dominant spirituality of a male-dominated institution.

How and whether to integrate this expanded awareness within the Christian symbology is the agenda of much feminist theology, which appropriately includes a thoroughgoing critique of Scripture and tradition. It has required of women the courage and the capacity to discern the actual lineaments and texture of their lived experience and their way of knowing and responding to the dimension of God in their lives. They have vividly communicated their sense that much of their lived experience is absent or denigrated in explicit and implicit meanings of the Christian tradition, with its dominantly male and heavily intellectualized modes of experiencing and responding to God. This realization has resulted in women paying attention to embodied experience and giving priority to its meanings rather than to the prescriptions mediated by males, for whom intellect and will are the primary modes of interaction with others and with the world at large.

Here can be seen an affinity between feminist and black spirituality. Black spirituality (acknowledging that sweeping generalizations are subject to many corrections) has emerged from and self-consciously reflected the lived experience of being sustained through unlimited oppression and suffering, and celebrating the One who sustains. This spirituality has been marked by a sense of identification with the black community and its history such that the individual's experience is important primarily in its reflection of and bondedness to the black community's experience.

In black spirituality, spiritual song and the reciprocally preached and heard word are modes of knowing as well as articulations of experience. Theology, in the analytical and abstracting mode of white European Christianity, is relativized in the black community. Priority of attention goes to lived experience and the expression of its meaning rather than to logical, analytical, and deductive reasoning from "correct" doctrinal formulations. The response tends to be more toward the biblical story than to doctrine. Story can be experienced, reexperienced, and lived. Doctrine tends to be thought.

This chapter began with a discussion of the differentiation of spirit from various psychological categories, coupled with the assertion that spirituality must not be viewed in isolation from the learnings of depth psychology. Among depth psychologies, it was maintained, ego psychology offers the most comprehensive view of the person. But it was indicated that ego psychology historically has been articulated implicitly within a positivistic philosophical orientation. But this orientation is not required by the psychology, nor is the epistemological structure of the separation of subject and object which is also assumed by most ego psychological theoreticians (Erikson being a more sophisticated exception).

Although it is possible to speak of a spirituality circumscribed by a positivistic philosophical orientation and founded on the separation of subject and object, it is clear that in this book spirituality refers to something else. Here the holistic vision of the person made possible by ego psychology is modified by the understanding of the human emerging from the phenomenology of religion and from the study of religious experience, including mysticism. These fields have long made clear what psychology has only now become able to accommodate theoretically through the concept of altered states of consciousness; that is, that reason and the five senses are not the only means of knowing reality, and that reality gives itself to be known through many modalities of lived experience. Such knowing occurs within cognitive and symbolic cultural structures, within patterns of relationships, and within types of action in the world. The capacity to perceive and respond to this other reality or other dimension of reality is what is meant by the concept of spirit. It can be understood as one of the many functions attributable to the concept "ego," an abstraction that incorporates numerous functions.

There are many different states of consciousness in which "ego" perceives and responds to reality, which is perceivable and conceptualizable in different modes, dimensions, or realms according to the state of consciousness in which the knowing occurs.

The radically altered states within mystical experience, however studied and respected, have never been normative in the history of Christian spirituality. Even St. Theresa, who acknowledged riches of knowing in advanced mystical states, advised those whom she instructed to "do whatsoever arouses you to love." Yet the Christian tradition has recognized that the quality of awareness and perception of "life in Christ Jesus" or "living in the presence of God" requires a movement from solitude to community with its shared life of relationships, liturgy (sacraments and preached word), and action in the world. These are all essential to maturing Christian spirituality.

How each person integrates these elements is precisely the ongoing quest of spiritual formation. There is no set answer or prescription of practice valid for everyone. "Integration" must be understood as process, not as achieved state. This is why images of movement, not attainment, are appropriate for Christian spirituality. "Journey," "pilgrimage," "spinning" and "weaving"—at times "wandering"—these are the metaphors of Christian spiritual formation.

In the next chapter we will examine the nature of the pastoral role and pastoral care as they apply to the concept of spirituality and the nurturing of its formation.

CHAPTER 3

A Theory of
Pastoral Care

Religion has been defined briefly as "a set of symbolic forms and acts which relate man to the ultimate conditions of his existence."[1] Religion is uniquely and essentially human. So, as Suzanne Langer[2] and others have clarified for us, the human being is the symbolizing being. To be human is to express experience symbolically. Religions are symbolic expressions of the human experience of engagement or relationship with a domain of power and meaning that transcends and undergirds and yet permeates the reality known to us through our "ordinary senses." Religions assert that human life is to be conducted as expressive of and conforming to the nature and requirements of this power and reality. Human life derives its meaning from this power and reality experienced always under particular social and historical conditions. Religious myths and rituals articulate the specific meanings of the power and reality. They express the relationship of the most significant aspects in the life of the particular human community to the power and reality experienced as ultimate by the community.

To put it briefly, religions declare what is real. As Mircea Eliade has taught us, religions express the human ontological quest for the "really real." By expressing/revealing human experience and its meaning, religious symbolizations enable the human to live in an ordered world, enable the human to transcend the mere givenness of sequential experience.

In the previous chapter we sought to establish the meanings of spirit and spirituality within an understanding of the human that takes seriously contemporary psychoanalytic thought, humanistic, transpersonal psychologies, and the psychology of consciousness. Two of three ways "spirit" has come to be used refer specifically to the human capacity for experience of, response to, participation in, and union with the transcendent. Religions articulate for humans the meanings of the transcendent and provide structures by means of which humans can grasp and organize their lives according to those meanings. In the broadest sense, this is the sphere of human existence to which "spirituality" refers. Religious systems tend to institutionalize leadership, and in the Christian tradition the religious leader is most commonly designated as pastor. In this chapter will be developed a broad understanding of pastoral care, to accommodate the breadth of the concept of spirituality.

Religious leaders are those persons whom the community has recognized as having particular gifts and experience that will enable them to enable the community to order its life so as to sustain the continuity between the way things ultimately are and the day-to-day experience of the community. "Continuity" has several meanings: (1) A community needs to understand its life as related to a structure of meaning and purpose. Here, the need for "continuity" refers to the ongoing need to have that relationship reaffirmed, reinterpreted, and continually made "plausible." (2) This becomes especially important at those points in individual or community life when unusual ("negative") events threaten the plausibility of the relationship. Death, illness, natural disasters, social crises such as conflict with other societies or defeat—all threaten the meaning, the world construction, according to which the community understands its life. (3) Another sphere in which the experience of continuity is maintained is in all those aspects of a community's life that are experienced and interpreted as reflecting basic relations in the ultimate order. Birth, the passage to adulthood, marriage, the planting and harvesting of the crops on which the community depends, the hunting of the animals on which the community depends—all of these crucial human actions need to be experienced in their continuity with the ultimate order of reality. Clifford Geertz has succinctly noted that religions provide models of and models for both the individual's and the community's life.[3]

When an individual, by virtue of personal characteristics, abilities, and experience is seen by the community as especially qualified to enable the community to sustain this social, cognitive, and affective continuity with the transcendent, he or she is set apart and trained for religious leadership. Pastoral care is one dimension of religous leadership, the essence of which is world construction and maintenance.

Through ritual, by interpreting natural or historical events, guiding its community's response to them, and by intervening in individual and familial situations of illness, distress, and conflict, religious leadership has always had the function of enabling the people to understand and experience their lives in openness to and continuity with the Sacred, by means of the given culture's symbolization of the Sacred. It must be understood that pastoral care functions to nurture absolutely basic, essential human actions: the construction, experience, and maintenance of an ordered, value-laden world, without which human beings risk losing their essential, distinctive humanness. In a differentiated culture like ours there are sources of meaning outside the religious structures and institutions. This condition of secularization tends to fragment experience, making it more difficult for persons to integrate the various aspects of their lives.

Also, the epistemological bias of modern science has put on the defensive those who would affirm the "objective pole" of religious experience. This has led to a tendency (not the rule in all sectors of contemporary society) to lose sensitivity to religious experience. Andrew Greeley[4] and others have noted that while large numbers of contemporary persons do have "mystical" experiences, many do not conceptualize these as "religious," in the sense of relating them to their particular religious institutions' symbol systems. The result is that the kind of experience that for eons has functioned to integrate the person psychologically within the religious symbol system and to validate the religious symbol system experientially is now too often experienced as merely anomalous.

In those church groups that have sought accommodation to modernity, pastoral care has tended to follow courses of action and self-understanding set by various psychotherapeutic systems. As we have seen, few of these systems gave serious consideration to the autonomous human need and capacity for a cognitively organized world and fewer still affirmed the epistemological significance of religious experience.

It is our position that the primary function of pastoral care is to enable persons in this postmodern era to experience and order their lives in openness to and according to the dimension of the Sacred Transcendent as manifest in the Judeo-Christian Scriptures, in the experience of the church through various traditions, and as it becomes revealed to the experience of church persons, in the very process of seeking this openness and order. In the broadest sense, this is Christian spiritual formation and it is the central task of pastoral care.

To emphasize the role of spirituality in pastoral care is to give prominence to the nurturing of this dimension of human consciousness and responsiveness in all spheres of pastoral care. The specifically Christian focus of spirituality happens because the nurturing occurs within the structure of Christian symbols. To see the nurturing of Christian spirituality as central to pastoral care is not, for example, to downplay the importance of crisis intervention in pastoral care, but rather to see that for the pastor, as contrasted with other mental health interventionists, the aim of intervention is not only restoration and strengthening of coping abilities (ego strength) but the utilization of the experience as a whole for deepening the person's consciousness of his or her life in its dimension of awareness of the responsiveness to "the actualization of power and meaning in unity," experienced and expressed in the context of Christian meanings. More specifically, the pastor's concern might be to enable the person to sense more clearly how his or her life was experienced and ordered according to actualizations of power and meaning that were destructive or inhibiting of more "valuable" or "worthy" power and meaning. In this case, growth in coping abilities would include an increased capacity in drawing on both the "teachings" and the sustaining power of which the church can be the vehicle.

Now this last formulation confronts us with the frankly metaphysical quality of pastoral care. The mark of modernity branded on the forehead of the liberal churches is the inability to experience, to let itself seek, be guided by, and to depend upon "the actualization of power and meaning in unity" for which "the Holy Spirit" is the Christian symbol. The Christian tradition has at times focused on "the power of God," "the power of Christ," "the spirit of Christ," as well as "the Holy Spirit," to articulate its experience of being led, guided by, admonished by, forgiven by, and sustained by an active, knowable, in some way personal "actualization of power and meaning in unity."

The hallmark of modernity has been the denial of metaphysical status to this experienced reality, and its explanation in terms of psychological or sociological processes which supposedly lend themselves to empirical or nontranscendent explanation. The recovery of spirituality in the sense of the experience of continuity between one's own deepest experience and the deepest, sustaining power and meaning of the universe is the most important task for contemporary pastoral care. For without this experience and the symbolization that enables its appropriation, religion is merely a collection of old stories and prescriptions for behavior reflecting the predilections of those who happen to endorse the religion.

Pastoral care must continue to be informed by depth psychology and what it has discovered about the psychological and developmental sources of the disturbance of persons and the ways in which humans use other persons and religious systems to compensate for the effects of these disturbances. Otherwise, religious leadership will continue to "dance around the bonfires of its own oedipal [and preoedipal] complex."[5] Contemporary pastoral care must continue to be informed by depth and ego psychology, but it must utilize these perspectives within a more adequate philosophical anthropology and theology, which take serious account of "spirit." Religious traditions have always recognized and made central these perceptions about human being: (1) its "original" or "primal" unity with the ultimately real; (2) its separation or alienation from the ultimately real; and (3) its most profound desire to be reunited with, reconciled with, or participate in, the ultimately real, the transcendent.

Religious symbolism is ambiguous; it closes off as well as opens up meaning. To utilize only one tradition of Christian theology, for example, is inevitably to diminish the range of experience to which the gospel has been addressed. Just so, to utilize only the language of the Christian tradition restricts the range of experience from which we can draw in order to understand our current situation and its possibilities. We need to be able to understand Christianity as organic to core human characteristics and capacities; if we can address our Christian categories only to those who already share our beliefs and vocabulary, then obviously we can only address each other. The result of this will be to narrow ineluctably the range of experience that we are aware of and can address; and sooner or later we find ourselves merely using familiar words, assuming a unanimity of experiential reference, with the gradual constriction of human experience so well exemplified by all self-satisfied, unreflective religious conservatism. Unless we can understand what human beings share in common, we cannot adequately appreciate the range of human experience that the gospel has addressed, nor adequately appreciate the apparently new human situation that currently confronts those who would by pastoring convey the gospel today.

The truth is that the Christian tradition has always affirmed that our human knowing and experience carry us ultimately into mystery. The realities we talk about are of a different order than those that intellect and speech can adequately grasp or describe. To claim definitive understanding is to delude oneself. To be content only with what is unequivocal is to condemn oneself to endless restlessness or to the stagnation of truncated truth. We need to heed the words of the anonymous author of *The Cloud of Unknowing,* who wrote concerning the realities of contemplative prayer that if we are to see or feel God in this life it must be in darkness or unknowing.[6]

Pastoral care must steer between the Scylla of constriction and the Charybdis of release.[7] It must not inappropriately attempt to control behavior and experience and thought, for the Spirit moves in ways that might at first seem inappropriate. On the other hand, it must not let itself drift into anomic chaos which affirms every inclination and idea as being ultimately of God and therefore equally to be indulged.

The pastor is a guide, both for the community as a whole and for the families and individuals who constitute the congregation. The image of guide is not drawn from the context of a tour on which there are specific sights to be pointed out and explained by the guide. Rather, the image of guide is drawn from that of guiding on an arduous journey, one that includes real danger and requires rigorous attention and commitment, but also promises great beauty, depths of satisfaction, intense enjoyment, wonder, and feelings of accomplishment and deep companionship.

In order to guide a congregation and the individuals within it the Christian pastor's life must be "spiritual." That is, his or her life must be characterized by attention and responsiveness to the domain of the "actualization of power and meaning in unity," the transcendent, as that is expressed and experienced in Christian symbols. This requires first of all a disciplined life of prayer, in which one's aim is attentiveness, openness, and receptivity to God, the ultimate context and power of being. "Whether you like it or not, read and pray daily. It is for your *life;* there is no other way; else you will be a trifler all your days. . . . Do justice to your own soul; give it time and means to grow. Do not *starve* yourselves any longer."[8] Prayer of this sort is much more than words spoken. Later in this work we will discuss various approaches to prayer, and provide a fuller rationale for the regular rigor of a life of prayer.

The pastor must have sensitive understanding of the experience of God revealed in the Bible. He or she must be capable of openness to being addressed by God in new ways in engagement with Scripture; and the pastor must be capable of empathy with the broadest possible range of human experience so as to enable the people to experience continuity between the dynamics of their own lives and the dynamics and purposes of the divine life. This assumes that the pastor has had the courage to explore his or her own reaches of brokenness, mystery, and joy. Only so can a pastor know deeply the continuity or engagement of Spirit to spirit, which it is his or her vocation to proclaim.

Because "spirituality" is corporate as well as individual, the pastor must understand liturgical and sacramental leadership in order that the gathered community may experience the Christian "actualization of power and meaning in unity" in their midst. Effective preaching reaches into the stories of the people, focuses on the deepest essentials, and connects this to the appropriate elements of God's story. In the joining of the stories, the union of power and meaning is made present and actual. Likewise, because the Judeo-Christian tradition experiences the active concern and presence of God in history, and this experience is of God's special concern for justice and liberation from oppression, so guidance in Christian spirituality includes enabling the community to engage in compassionate social action for justice and liberation. That is to say, Christian "spiritual experience" or "knowledge of God" or "encounter with Christ" will be severely truncated and thereby distorted if we do not undertake actions analogous to those cited by Isaiah and referred by Jesus to his own life and ministry in his reading in the synagogue reported in Luke 4.

Such then, in sketch, is the association between spirituality and pastoral care. Obviously, this understanding of spirituality differs from notions of spirituality confined to images of privatized pietism, or from a life of prayer detached from engagement in the world; and it suggests continuity with non-Christians and even non-"religious" spirituality, while suggesting the importance of the distinctiveness of Christian spirituality.

The view of pastoral care that informs this work differs from that of William Clebsch and Charles Jaekle, who see pastoral care primarily as response to "troubled persons." They say, "Pastoral care begins when an individual person recognizes or feels that his trouble is unsolvable in the context of his own private resources, and when he becomes willing, however subconsciously, to carry his hurt and confusion to a person who represents to him, however vaguely, the resources, and wisdom and authority of religion."[9]

Pastoral care is care taken by the pastor not only for the healing, guidance, reconciliation, and sustaining of souls who recognize themselves as troubled persons. Pastoral care is also care taken for the nurturing, guidance, and growth of persons in relationship to themselves, others, nature, and God,[10] as an ongoing part of ministry unrelated to whether the person experiences himself or herself in crisis or in trouble.

Whereas Don Browning (in the most important book on pastoral care in the past decade) wishes to emphasize the importance of "socializ[ing church] members into a distinctive style of life"[11] as the aim of pastoral care, in this book the focus of pastoral care is on the "consciousness," the experience of the church member. More particularly, the focus is on the formation of a consciousness that can be experienced and articulated in a variety of ways: the sense of the presence of God, the continuity between the human and the divine, the encounter with Christ, life in Christ Jesus, the spiritual Presence, the power of the Holy Spirit, relationship with God, the life of Christ. I do not believe these to be equivalent symbols; they point to differing emphases of experience. But they all have legitimacy, and for reasons not fully clear but not accidental, different formulations are felt to be particularly appropriate by different persons. The development of this dimension of experience is essential. For without this awareness there is no experiential base for commitment to Christ and the church; membership becomes a matter of mere fellowship, intellectual agreeability, or solely a matter of the will.

In their appropriate concern to be open to the claims of the disciplines of modernity and to be effective in the area of charity and social justice, so-called liberal churches have neglected the nurture and development of the experiential base of religion, which is an essential element of holistic spirituality.

Recent attention to the structure and dynamics of faith de-velopment[12] and the rediscovery of the Christian tradition of spiritual direction[13] have made us more clearly cognizant that "spiritual formation" is a lifelong process toward which we can be intentional and disciplined, without being restrictive or controlling. "Spiritual formation" is our phrase to point to what should be the ongoing development of a deepening ex-perience of one's life in its relationship to the transcendent. It is simultaneously a process of self-discovery, engagement with others, and a deepening and broadening of one's discovery of relationship to or participation in the transcendent.

Now this is not simply a process of consciousness expansion. It is a process that results in and is shaped by one's response in the actions of one's life. As an able pastor has formulated it, "The world, its needs and conditions, shapes the formation of [one's] spiritual life in accordance with his involvement in its redemption."[14] But many Christians have discovered that years of active attention to redemptive action in the world without attention to the ongoing engagement of spirit and Spirit have resulted in a sense of aimlessness, uncenteredness, and the experience of estrangement of their inner being from God's sustaining Spirit. The Religious Society of Friends, Sojourners, and the Church of the Savior in Washington, D.C., are examples of Christian communities that attempt to hold in creative balance the complementarity of solitary and corporate spiritual nurturing, and action in the world that is expressive of and yet also influences the spirituality of the individual mem-bers and the body.

Spirituality is by no means an exclusively Christian dimen-sion of experience. It is a function of distinctly human being and is a part of all cultures, in various (fulfilling and distorting) manifestations. Herein lies one of contemporary Western Christianity's greatest evangelical opportunities. For a variety of reasons, including the rise of awareness of Eastern religions, altered states of consciousness, stress, relaxation, and meditation, ecological concerns, our culture is "tuning in" on inner experience. Some of this is healthy, some is pathologically narcissistic. Here Gresham's law of economics, that bad currency drives out good, suggests a danger also in the realm of culture. But this makes the present time an opportune moment for pastors who have had serious, disciplined experience in spiritual formation. For such pastors will be able to recognize in these non-Christian and even non-"religious" types of spirituality adumbrations and analogies of the experience familiar to Christians and expressed in Christian symbols.

Pastors whose own spirits have been responsive to the movement of the Spirit outside of narrow Christian contexts are able both to elicit and respond to spiritual yearnings nascent in their congregations as well as in persons outside their congregations. Thus an approach to pastoral care sensitive to inner experience can be of strong evangelistic significance, without the exclusive evangelical restriction to the inculcation of feelings of guilt, fear, and forgiveness.

In fact, persons experience deep rootedness and participation in and communion with the source of power and meaning in a myriad of contexts: moments in the Eucharist, in nature, childbirth, suffering for justice, admiring art, shared action for social betterment, to name only a few. The work of pastoral care includes recognizing these human experiences as responses to the Holy Spirit, empathically interpreting and naming them as such while affirming their integrity in themselves, and guiding persons so that they may know these spirit-moments as integral to life in Christ Jesus.

CHAPTER 4

The Function of Prayer in Spiritual Formation

It is a curious comment on the state of religion in our culture that among religious professionals one must make a case for prayer. Years of conversations with pastors of mainline Protestant denominations leave no doubt, however, that many pastors are at least uninformed about prayer, often suspicious, and more than occasionally downright hostile to discussing prayer. The ignorance, suspicion, and hostility one encounters is not accidental, nor is it necessarily due to the character structure of the person involved. There are historical, sociological, and theological reasons for persons' objections to prayer. Let us examine some of them.

Works Righteousness

Protestantism is rooted in Martin Luther's reaction against what has come to be called works righteousness. He challenged the Catholic Church's odious practice of indulgences, and he experienced the ultimate futility of trying to wrest the experience of forgiveness from God through ascetical practices, including prayer.

Luther validated a Christian calling to be in the world, which undermined the notion that the monastery provided the context and structure in which one most appropriately carries on the relationship to God. The monasteries were above all places of prayer, so again, Luther's action called prayer as a vocation into question, and by extension (in recent times) all prayer outside of corporate liturgy.

Proclamation

In addition, over the centuries Luther's emphasis on faithful proclamation and reception of the Word, combined with the Calvinist emphasis on correct doctrine and teaching, has developed in many Protestants the assumption that the center of spiritual activity is the preaching and hearing of the Word by the corporate body, not prayer in solitude. Much of liberal Protestantism has imitated the Calvinistic focus on the intellect, to the neglect of more intuitive, receptive forms of interior life.

Social Concerns

In recent decades, many of the liberal Protestant clergy have been in self-conscious or unconscious revolt against what they experience as the authoritarian self-righteousness of their pietistic forebears, for whom, as they were rightly or wrongly perceived, the saying of prayers went along with a narrow moralism unconcerned with broader issues of oppression and social justice.

Many of today's most effective Protestant clergy were trained under the influence of the rational propheticism of the Niebuhrs, Paul Tillich, and their colleagues. The focus of these theologians on the social order made the interpretation of social dynamics on the basis of historical-critical interpretation of Scripture and the bending of the will toward justice the center and circumference of spirituality. Prayer was seen as privatized, escapist, self-indulgent, and—one may venture— feminine. One of these committed and effective pastors told me that in the late 1950s, one of his professors was asked why he did not begin each class with a prayer, as some other faculty members did. The professor replied, "Gentlemen, if your whole life is not a prayer, then you have no business being here in the first place." Aside from the arrogance of his implicit claim that his entire life was one of devotion, this teacher's focus on the external world of action and—presumably— thought, to the exclusion of structured times of solitary prayer, typifies the response of many of the finest of that generation of theological teachers under whom so many contemporary clergy were trained.

Depth Psychology

An additional factor underlying much skepticism regarding prayer is the influence of depth psychology in theological education in the past three decades. This is a story permeated by ambiguity, but one result has been to direct the attention of those who *were* drawn to interiority and receptivity as modes of spirituality to disciplines of sheerly subjective experience. Breakthroughs of meaning and grace are not unknown in the process of psychotherapy, but the structure hardly lends itself to their interpretation as engagement with the Holy Spirit, except in the most attenuated terms. Furthermore, the overall effect was to reinforce the belief of the "externalizers" that curiosity about the interior was a neurotic manifestation, and the best to be hoped for was that when the neurotic itch got scratched, the person would be freed up for social action.

Clinical Pastoral Education

Along with the influence of psychoanalytic theory came the development of clinical modalities of pastoral intervention in theological education. Clinical pastoral education (CPE) be- came mandatory for ordination in some denominations, and most mainline liberal seminaries encouraged their students to enroll for a clinical quarter at some point during their semi- nary careers. As one whose life was changed by CPE, I have neither the wish nor the intention to denigrate this fundamen- tally important advance in education for ministry. But it is widely recognized within the CPE movement itself that the combination of the comprehensive antireligious bias of psychoanalytic theory and the success of the clinical model diverted attention from traditional practices of formation such as prayer, meditation, and Bible study.

There is no need to denigrate these tendencies within Protestantism. It denies no credit to its exponents for what they accomplished to point out that the accomplishment has been won to the exclusion of much that has been profound in the history of the Christian experience of God, and the exclusion of dimensions of one's own being. The epidemic of midlife crisis, burnout, and the experience of meaninglessness in ministry suggests that we neglect the interior firming of our connectedness and relationship with the Ultimate only at great risk to ourselves.

Obviously, the human being is more than intellect and will, which have been the main elements of human psychology to which modern liberal Protestantism has been attentive. Religion and spirituality have to do not only with intellect and volition, but also with behavior, affect, intuition, and aesthetic sensibility. The full human being creates and responds to the world on the basis of a diversity of "mental" and sensory capabilities. The response to the world and the effect of the world's response upon the person alters or reinforces the basic way in which the person understands and interprets reality. Prayer, as an action of more than intellect and will, can play a crucial role in the construction and experience of reality. The following section will describe the relationship between prayer and the construction/experience of reality, which is what is meant by "consciousness."

Because the language of the psychology of consciousness will be employed to describe this aspect of the human reality, it is necessary to describe what is meant by "consciousness." This term eludes precise definition while nevertheless being a crucial element of human being. Regarding the difficulty of defining the term, a recent author has written,

> Consciousness, defined by Locke as "the perception of what passes in man's own mind," is recognized today as a multifaceted, multidimensional concept. There is no agreement about its boundaries or how it works or how to study it. The various interpretations of consciousness can be held in mind as potentially fruitful hypotheses pending the accumulation of convincing evidence that supports one particular view.[1]

Consciousness refers to how we construct, experience, and respond to our world. Consciousness includes the stream of our thoughts and feelings, our awareness of this stream, and our awareness of being aware. The process of constructing our consciousness is identical with constructing our sense of "reality." We cannot know "external" reality in itself; we can only "know" it through the contents of our own consciousness. Robert Ornstein has described the process this way: "Sense organs gather information that the brain can modify and sort. This heavily filtered input is compared with memory, expectations, body movements, and until, finally, our consciousness is constructed as a 'best guess' about reality. These 'best guesses' are the formations of our assumptive world; they offer stability at the cost of exclusion."[2]

The exclusion occurs because our brain filters out information that has no survival value. We are not fully aware at any moment of all the processes that involve our sensory receptors. By focusing our attention we can become aware of various processes, but at no time can our personal consciousness "fully represent the external world or even our internal world but must consist of an extremely small fraction of the entire 'reality.'"[3]

Cultures and subcultures are bound together by the sharing of constructions of reality on the basis of consensus. Of course, one's consciousness is a primary datum of experience, is subjective, and in itself is not available to others for observation. Thus language takes on enormous importance in the construction and maintenance of shared reality, since it is the main vehicle by means of which persons communicate with each other about (ultimately) subjective experience. Furthermore, language is not only a means of communication but also takes on a structuring function, since it both forms and interprets sensory perception, emotional response, and so on.

In fact, we are born into a context of shared meaning, and language both shapes and conveys the meanings shared within a culture. Although another's consciousness in itself may not be available to us, because a common language and structure of meaning shape and permeate all the consciousness of a culture, we therefore do have a basis for our sense of the possibility of understanding another.

It is evident that an individual's construction of reality is a matter of consciousness, and that the consciousness is constructed out of physical, cognitive, affective, and relational experience. Chronic malnutrition, for example, will create cognitive distortions; poor children perceive nickels to be physically larger than they actually are.[4]

A culture is a group that shares a given construction of reality (understanding, of course, that there are always individual modifications of any cultural assumptions and systems). Reality is established on the basis of consensus and maintained by common language and reinforcing behavior. "Reality" includes an interpretation of the "objective" world, the philosophical assumptions that support that interpretation, cultural and social structures and values, shared moral imperatives, and so on. The list could go on but is sufficient to convey the complexity of the notion of reality and the force it has in establishing and maintaining what is "real." Our cultural assumptions tend to support a view of reality that denigrates states of consciousness that claim to inform us about reality that is not symmetrical with the reality assumed by our techno-scientific outlook.

With all of this cultural influence on the formation and maintenance of consciousness and its assumptive definition of reality, we can describe the primary function of Christian spiritual disciplines to be the development of a consciousness influenced by the symbols, myths, rituals, actions, and meanings of the historical Christian community. Through spiritual discipline we aim to let our consciousness be influenced by the view of reality and values communicated in Scripture, sacrament, preached Word, and Christian action in the world, all of which together form the context within which we pray.

The concepts of spirituality and spirit pertain to the whole of Christian life. The Christian spiritual tradition has always asserted that even those called to be mystics must structure their prayer within the context of the whole of Christian life. This means regular participation in the liturgy and Eucharist, study of Scripture, hearing the preached Word, communications with the community, acts of charity, and so on. The tradition has always affirmed what we would today call a "holistic" view of spirituality. Although this book emphasizes prayer, it must be repeated that prayer is not the sole locus of spirituality.

Spiritual discipline, then, is not limited to solitude. All of these other elements are essential to the disciplined religious life. Nevertheless, solitude has an essential role to play. In committing ourselves to the discipline of regular solitude, we place ourselves in the consciousness-context of the reality we affirm in the liturgy and in the community of Christians. We stand before or within this reality just as ourselves; it is an act of trust and commitment in which we attempt to open ourselves to the address (not to be literally understood as verbal) of the One in whom we live and move and have our being.

John Cobb has said about prayer in solitude that there is "no other way to achieve adequate self-knowledge, self-control and

stability of commitment. . . . With others there are always intervening variables to honesty, but thinking of oneself as alone
before God enables and causes us to take a deeper responsibility for ourselves."[5] Cobb's observation is focused on self-
knowledge and will, but these too have an important role to
play in the maintenance of a reality-construction. In the next
sections we will see in more detail how specific disciplines of
prayer function to sustain and enrich the Christian experience
and construction of reality.

To recapitulate somewhat, pastoral care was defined in relation to world-construction and maintenance. In this section,
the focus has been on consciousness as the construction of
reality, another way of talking about world-construction. The
Christian church affirms the *reality* of what it symbolizes by
God, Christ, Jesus, Holy Spirit. It affirms that these symbols
point to the ultimate context and power of our being and that
we can participate in and be engaged by this power. Symbols
function to open us to this reality and thereby serve as vehicles
for its power or influence upon us. These affirmations find
little support in the culture of modernity. And, in fact, day-to-
day, ordinary life in most cultures is not sufficient to sustain
such a religious consciousness. All religions have recognized
the need for spiritual practices in order to keep the culture and
its individuals open to the specific definition of reality affirmed
by the religious system.

Spirit and spirituality, the capacity for experiencing relatedness to the transcendent, are fundamental human categories.
The discussion of consciousness brings the concepts of spirit
and spirituality closer to the descriptive categories of the
human sciences and out of the rarefied, too often disembodied
realm of theological discourse. But on the other hand, we can
also see that the human sciences themselves occur within a
broader philosophical horizon, their specific theories inevitably resting upon assumptions about the Real.

A study of consciousness shows that the Real never is known apart from culturally influenced structures of knowing. This is true even in the physical sciences, much more so in the human sciences, and even more in the area of cultural meanings and values. The Judeo-Christian tradition has been formed through diverse historical and cultural conditions and influenced by many different philosophical orientations. Its symbols are many, complex, and multivalent, accommodating to these various historical, cultural, and philosophical conditions. We do not learn about or experience reality except through symbolic forms and acts. Unless these symbols are effectively related to experience, unless they both illuminate, confirm, and order experience, they lose their power. Conversely, the meanings borne by symbols, the reality they point to and participate in, must be experienced, lived. The heart of the Christian pastor's responsibility is to relate persons' experience to the realities conveyed by Christian symbols. Only through experience can their truth be transformatively known. As will be shown, the disciplines of prayer provide structures through which such experience may happen.

TYPES OF PRAYER

Prayer is the focused endeavor to open our awareness to the reality of the transcendent. This is not to say that only in moments of private prayer can we become open in this way. Quite the contrary; for the Christian the receiving of the sacraments and the hearing of the preached Word have always been recognized as essential for opening us in this way. "Means of grace" means that such actions become vehicles for the awareness of the presence of God, or the actions of God in our experience. And as was acknowledged earlier, action in participation with the poor and oppressed is also recognized as essential to the deepened awareness of and receptivity to the transcendent God.

Nevertheless, spiritual formation requires prayer in solitude. As quoted earlier, John Cobb has written that "thinking of ourselves as alone before God enables and causes us to take a deeper responsibility for ourselves."[6] It also enables an alteration from our ordinary, task-oriented, day-to-day state of consciousness, influenced primarily by our need to maintain our self-image and respond to the expectations of others upon us.

Centering Prayer

Solitude is the withdrawal pole of the withdrawal-engagement rhythm that characterizes mature spirituality. Evelyn Underhill has written that "as your meditation becomes deeper it will defend you from the perpetual assaults of the outer world. You will hear the busy hum of that world as a distant exterior melody, and know yourself to be in some sort withdrawn from it. You have set a ring of silence between you and it; and behold! within that silence you are free."[7] But this withdrawal is not automatic. The "outer world" that Underhill refers to is very much a part of our "inner world." One reason why attempts to establish ordered prayer life fail is because sitting down in solitude to "pray" is experienced as no more than (and no less than) an implosion of our ordinary involvement and concerns about ourselves and about the "outer world," but in a condition of immobility. At least if we are up and about we can have the sense of doing something about these concerns (or at least doing something to avoid them).

The issue, then, is how to develop a consciousness conducive to "effective" experiencing of ourselves and our concerns in the outer world. This should not be confused with creating a consciousness that avoids these issues through blissful unawareness. Such approaches to prayer and meditation are rightfully criticized by proponents of the active life. But such approaches by no means exhaust the field of possibility in prayer.

Establishing this context of consciousness is the function of what has been called "centering" prayer. Most serious schools of prayer have some procedure by means of which this "ring of silence" can be drawn, this shift of consciousness can be effected. Underhill suggests that the would-be meditator fix the attention upon an object (either external or mental) and hold the object fast in attention. Such an object might be the plaster or mental image of a saint, a brief verse of Scripture, or a word like "love" or "peace." The meditator is instructed to stay focused on the object, rejecting and thwarting all attempts of the wayward mind to distract the attention away from the object and toward the concerns of self and/or outer world.

Another approach is to repeat silently or vocally a short word or phrase. This is what the Sanskrit word "mantra" refers to. Whereas Underhill urges the meditator to do battle against all distracting thoughts, this approach instructs the meditator not to try to keep out thoughts, feelings, and images, but that when one becomes aware that one's mind has in fact wandered, when the attention has been distracted, then the meditator gently but firmly turns the attention back to the object of meditation.

The most easily learned and widely effective approach that I have used and taught is a simple breath-counting procedure. The meditator sits erect and relaxed, closes the eyes, and becomes attentive to the breathing. After a few moments, on the exhale the meditator says to himself or herself, "one"; inhales and exhales; and on the exhale says, "two"; inhale, exhale—"three"; inhale, exhale—"four." Then the procedure is repeated, counting silently on the exhale, one, two, three, four. When one becomes aware that one's mind has wandered from the breath-counting, one brings the attention back to it. One does not try to keep out any thoughts or feelings or images, only to be alert and focused on the breathing. And when one realizes that the attention has wandered, one brings the attention back to the counting.

It is obvious that in this procedure one is not concerned with pious thoughts, or with attaining any kind of enlightenment, receiving visions, or hearing voices. One is only instructed to pay attention and to be alert when one has ceased paying attention and to bring the mind back to attention directed where the will intends. There is no opportunity here for self-congratulation, since "doing" this meditation without the mind wandering is virtually impossible.

This meditation procedure begins with an essential human problem, our distractedness of mind, feelings, and heart. It recognizes that our ordinary day-to-day consciousness is probably more often responding to demands and expectations of others (real or imagined on our part) or to that endless inner stream of worries, agendas, regrets, hopes, anxieties, plans, and irritations, which make up our ordinary moment-to-moment stream of consciousness. In this sense, we do not belong to ourselves. We belong to the agendas we perceive from the outer world and to that preconscious clatter of concerns that bring themselves to our unattended awareness and make themselves the center of our preoccupation. Our ordinary day-to-day state of consciousness tends to be, to a great extent, captive to these concerns.

Centering meditation is the first step in the day-in and day-out effort to transform our ordinary day-to-day consciousness and open it so that it may be more alert to the presence of the transcendent. This procedure has several effects. It is physically relaxing and resting. It therefore is restorative and healing in the physical sense. But because it is physically relaxing and because we are embodied persons, the physical relaxation tends to make us more relaxed emotionally, less tense and anxious, more at home in, and therefore more at one with, the world.

Another effect it has is paradoxical. Inevitably, our mind wanders, in directions we do not select, to images and feelings, and thoughts and preoccupations that emerge unbidden into our awareness and capture our attention. We very quickly become aware of how distracted we are, how little we are in control of our most personal psychological processes, our consciousness. We are immediately confronted by our inability to do what we have set out to do—pay attention to our breath—and are in fact subject to all those thoughts and feelings that can emerge from nowhere but ourselves; and since they do, they cannot but represent who we are. The fact that they captivate our attention is indicative of the degree to which we are attached to them, not only in the moment but as a fact of our inner identity. This is humbling. It can also be experienced as infuriating and depressing. The paradox is that in experiencing our distractedness we in fact become more integrated. That is to say, by permitting these to emerge into our awareness we become more open to our own inner processes, to who we actually are.

In this centering meditation, we cannot attribute these distractions to anybody else; they are ours, they are us. There is no one whom we can blame for our inability to keep our attention on our breath. We must take responsibility for these distractions, even as we are instructed not to become attached to them. We might be dismayed by our captivation by them, but meditating makes it impossible for us to live under the illusion that we are free of them. For they inevitably do reflect who we are, our preoccupations, our needs for recognition and scapegoats, our guilts, anxieties, hopes, plans, affections—the stuff of our subjective identity.

We discover unpredicted angers, fears, and temptations. We discover that we envy those we respect, resent those who are benevolent to us. Most persons' attempts to establish an ongoing discipline of prayer founder because they are not instructed in a range of procedures that can keep them growing. On coming face to face with their own guilt, depression, anger, or boredom, they become discouraged and give up. Thus does the pain of self-encounter make discipline difficult. As Saint Teresa of Avila warned, in the "early stage, as the soul is still absorbed in worldly affairs, engulfed in worldly pleasure, and puffed up with worldly honors and ambitions, its vessels, which are the senses and the faculties given to it by God as part of its nature, have not the same power, and such a soul is easily vanquished, although it may desire not to offend God and may perform good works."[8]

Self-discovery of this sort is, of course, an ongoing experience in prayer. A serious prayer life does not lend itself to an experience of sinlessness or perfection. Quite the contrary, what is most frequently discovered is one's ignorance, one's inability even to pay attention to the focus of prayer, let alone in life manifest its virtues.

It is for this reason that criticisms of sustained attention to prayer as being self-indulgence or avoidance of reality are off the mark. True, much prayer may be self-indulgent, just as much action in the world may be attempts at self-justification through works righteousness. But serious prayer is precisely an encounter with reality—initially an encounter with one's own very finite and imperfect reality, experienced with painful particularity. It is for this reason that, especially in the beginning stages, a supportive and knowledgeable teacher and support group are vital.

Engaging these elements of ourselves can be dismaying to beginners who think that once they start "praying" they should experience primarily feelings of closeness to God or relationship to Jesus. When they discover that they in fact confront their own anxieties, guilts, griefs, or simply woolgathering, they tend to feel inadequate (and resentful) or unworthy in God's eyes, since they are not being rewarded for their efforts. In this regard, Thomas Merton has written: "Far from establishing one in unassailable narcissistic security, the way of prayer brings us face to face with the sham and indignity of the false self that seeks to live for itself alone and to enjoy the 'consolation of prayer' for its own sake."[9]

Pastors who want to help persons grow by means of a significant prayer life would be well-advised to remind them that the tradition has always asserted that "purgation" is an essential and inevitable dimension of serious prayer. It is also a part of the wisdom of the tradition that there is no knowledge of God without knowledge of the self. A simple procedure like breath counting enables these essential elements of the spiritual life to occur.

In my teaching of seminary students, pastors, and members of congregations, I always begin with the breath counting rather than have them "meditate" on words or phrases from Scripture or words like "peace," because these words still suggest that there ought to be a particular kind of experience to accompany or result from the meditation. It sets up expectations. The breath counting deprives us of the familiarity of religious phrases, the self-induced comfort or conflict that they can provide.

The issue is not how to help persons feel more secure, more taken care of; this can be accomplished more effectively by self-hypnotic techniques available through cassettes, secular adult education programs, and so forth. The issue is how to enable persons to develop and maintain procedures that can enable their lifelong spiritual formation. Learning how to pay attention, to bring the will to bear on what the heart intends; being humble enough to learn about and accept one's own finitude, to be open and receptive to that—these are fundamental to serious spiritual growth.

Our religious attention is too likely to be captured by our desires for our own self-enhancement. We have a long agenda of what we want from God by way of good feelings, affirmation, assurance, consolation for our miseries, compensation for our renunciations, clear guidance about what we should do, and on and on. We are filled with our own desires, our own needs for self-importance, our need to feel safe and protected.

A centering meditation like breath counting is foundational to spiritual formation because it is an act of trust, acceptance, and humility. It is saying with our body and our will, heart, and mind that we are willing to encounter how vulnerable we are to these dimensions of our being, how easily our will is distracted, how little our attention is under our control.

Now perhaps some comments are in order about "attention." To pay attention to another is the most complete gift of ourselves we can give short of our life itself. Genuinely to pay attention is to let our consciousness be totally given over to the other. To pay attention fully is to have no thoughts about what I would rather be doing, or what I want from this relationship, or about what I ought to be saying. To pay attention is to be empty of my own project for the moment. It is not just to make a place in my awareness for the other; it is to turn my awareness over to the other, to be hospitable in the fullest possible way. If I am counseling, I become poor; that is, I put aside the riches of my theoretical knowledge, my images of health and sickness, my notions of what is right and wrong about and for the other person, and simply turn my attention over to the other. It is safe to venture that we seldom manage moments of attention such as these.

This casts an interesting light on, for example, our receptivity to God as evidenced by how we make hospitable space for God in hearing the Word in Scripture read in an ordinary church service. How little we are able to pay attention. Most of us are rarely fully open to the Word, fully attentive as it is read in church or in our private devotions. We can barely conceive what it might mean to be fully, undistractedly attentive for fifteen seconds. Even if we think we are paying attention, what we are likely to be doing is fitting what we are hearing into our preexistent understanding of the passage, or immediately trying to apply it to whatever happens to be on our mind at the moment; or we are silently congratulating ourselves on *our* deep understanding and reception of the passage (and wishing so-and-so would take it to heart and thereby stop being such a pain). But seldom do we simply open ourselves to be fully attentive and receive the Word. In fact, we may not even know what that might mean. How can we simply receive the Word? Isn't the whole process of cognition and understanding dependent on the reception and organization of new information according to the preexistent schemata of our mind?

Yes, exactly, and this is another reason why it makes sense to found our prayer life on a procedure that works toward, even though it never fully accomplishes, freeing us from these preexistent structures that distort even as they accommodate the Word of God happening at any given moment. This is why learning to pay attention through this procedure of meditation is essential for the spiritual life. If we believe that God is the One in whom we live and move and have our being, from whose presence we are never separated, whose *davar* ("word," in Hebrew) is not only spoken or written word, but also event, happening, or even experience, then—to say the least—it behooves us to learn to pay attention each moment of our lives.

There are other procedures, easily learned, that perform a centering function. One is similar to the breath counting, but instead of counting breaths, the instructions are simply to be aware of and pay attention to one's inhaling and exhaling. Some persons prefer the breath counting because the combination of paying attention to the breath and to the counting gives them a little more to do; others are quite comfortable with the less busy action of simply being attentive to the breath.

Another centering procedure that aims at the combination of relaxation, receptiveness, attentiveness, and centeredness is to count one's thoughts. In this procedure, one sits quietly with the eyes closed and counts every thought that comes to mind.

Any content of consciousness is to be regarded as a thought. Thus any feeling, any fantasy, image, or sound that one becomes aware of is regarded as a thought and is counted like the others. This exercise trains one to pay attention and to become more aware of each item of experience.

There is a fourth procedure that many find helpful in centering. This is a prayer of great significance and power in the Christian tradition, the Jesus Prayer. Including it among centering procedures is subject to disagreement, since for some the Jesus Prayer is *the* central prayer. Readers familiar with *The Way of the Pilgrim*[10] remember that the pilgrim's entire spirituality was centered upon the Jesus Prayer and emerged from its effect upon the pilgrim. And in the Greek Orthodox tradition the Jesus Prayer was central to the development of the monk's prayer life. Purists might feel that there is something almost blasphemous about including the Jesus Prayer among other centering procedures.

Nevertheless, because so many have found centeredness and integration deepening through working with this as a centering prayer, I will describe it here as well as discuss it later when we consider apophatic prayer. The words of the complete Jesus Prayer are "Lord Jesus Christ, Son of God, have mercy on me, a sinner." These phrases are said with attention to each word, the first phrase being spoken (or thought) on the inhale, the second on the exhale, the third on the inhale, and the fourth on the exhale. The instructions are not to let oneself think discursively about the meaning(s) of the prayer, not to get carried away by the immensity of the concepts, but simply to say the prayer to oneself in rhythm with the breathing. One should focus one's attention on the prayer, being fully receptive to each word and phrase.

As in any centering procedure, the mind tends to become distracted. When one realizes that one has become distracted, the mind is brought gently back to focus on the words of the prayer. The words are to be said simply, without an attempt to evoke any particular feeling. In this way, one cannot indulge oneself in the self-gratifying flights of association or feeling that could so easily be stirred by words so powerful. Rather, one is called on to have a different sort of mind; one is simply attentive to the words, without associating to them one's own meanings and reactions. This is certainly a different way of being present to these words than we would ordinarily assume.

In saying the prayer in this manner, one is devoted entirely to the words, not to one's own piety, associations, or deep thinking. Reciting the prayer is simultaneously an act of humility and the kind of reverence that the increasing capacity for attention makes possible. But again, any kind of focus on feeling constitutes a distraction from the simple saying of the prayer. Writing of the Jesus Prayer, George Maloney says, "It can . . . serve as a preparation for prayer in order to integrate us, to pull us together and reach that 'still point,' deep within where we know he lives and loves us."[11] While distractions in the form of reflections about the life of Jesus or the various meanings of the prayer may be present for the beginner, over time one becomes more able just to be with the prayer, without associations, images, and so on.

This is the process that the Russian Orthodox teachers mean by descending into the heart. The image here is of depth; in prayer one aims to move toward the innermost depths of oneself, toward the heart which is, as Merton has described it, beneath the level of personality itself and its images, thoughts, and attachments. The "heart" can be spoken of as the meeting place of Spirit and spirit, where we experience our oneness with God. As Henri Nouwen has described it, the heart is "that point of our being where there are no divisions or distinctions and where we are totally one."[12]

The tradition of the Jesus Prayer has been joined to the tradition of the Prayer of the Heart in Greek Orthodox and

Russian spirituality. They come together in the following way. The Jesus Prayer, so the tradition teaches, leads us deep within ourselves and develops within us so as to emerge from our depths. It both leads to the heart and is an expression of the heart. But the Prayer of the Heart is regarded in the tradition as primarily a prayer of inner silence, empty of words, concepts, or images. It is what the Western tradition has called contemplative prayer.

The great Russian Orthodox master Theophan the Recluse wrote, "We must acquire the habit of always being in communion with God, without any image, any process of reasoning, any perceptible movement of thought. Such is the true expression of prayer. The essence of inner prayer, or standing before God with the mind in the heart, consists precisely in this."[13] From this perspective we can see how acquiring this inner state of consciousness can be related to an apophatic understanding of God.

The refusal to dwell on thoughts, feelings, or images of God, but rather to know God in a state of consciousness in which these play no part, makes possible an apprehension of God as being utterly beyond any thoughts we can have of God, or any characteristics or qualities we might attribute to God. This is the apophatic way. Of course, in reflecting on this kind of prayer, phrases to characterize the experience are used, such as God's love and God's Presence, the Presence of Christ abiding within us, and so on. In fact, the language of the desert Fathers and Mothers and of the Hesychasts tends to be extremely lush and personal in describing their relationship to the persons of the Trinity. But all the colorful and loving images are envisioned against the backdrop of silence and emptiness, for which the desert itself was their primary image.

Apophatic spirituality is by no means limited to the Orthodox tradition. Meister Eckhart's emphasis on poverty and indifference (detachment) as essential for knowing the

Godhead behind God reflects a similar apophatic spirituality. The same could be said about the anonymous English author of *The Cloud of Unknowing,* who wrote, "Therefore I will leave on one side everything I can think, and choose for my love that thing which I cannot think! Why? Because he may well be loved, but not thought. By love he can be caught and held, but by thinking never."[14]

For this author, "love" refers to the profound yearning to be joined to the infinite God beyond all comprehension. His instructions include the admonition to discover that center of yearning for union deep within one and to let oneself be totally caught up in that yearning, eschewing all thoughts and images, to be totally one with the yearning for union, which is love. There is an evident correspondence here between this author's instructions and the instruction of Theophan the Recluse, who wrote, "If feeling towards God is born and lives in your heart, then you will possess unceasing prayer."[15] Elsewhere, Theophan wrote, "Descend with the mind into the heart, and there stand before the face of the Lord, ever-present, all seeing, within you."[16] Of course, the author of *The Cloud of Unknowing* and Theophan share in the Platonic, pseudo-Dionysius philosophical-mystical tradition, so it is not surprising that there would be these similarities.

Such prayer makes great demands. Church persons are generally familiar with the fact that St. Anthony was tempted in the desert. What is less well-known is that the intense encounter with the wild beasts of the desert was a metaphor for the frightening encounter with the beasts within. Although the spirituality of the desert Fathers and Mothers was marked ultimately by a profound sense of abiding in God, and the peace and stability of that wordless and imageless assurance, the way there is the way of brutal self-encounter.

In the desert there is no recourse to the familiar, comforting structures of civilization, none of the diversions of daily life that permit us to hide from our inmost selves. The apophatic way, even in the instructions in prayer, requires a letting go of all attachment to what gratifies the ego, whether it be titles, learning, gifts, accomplishments, charity, intellect, or imagination—all must be let go of as one moves ever deeper toward the inner empty place of the spaciousness of God.

The author of *The Cloud of Unknowing* warns that any thought, whether of our own sinfulness or of "God's sweetness and love,"[17] leads away from God, and we become "disintegrated beyond belief!"[18]

The rigor of this approach tends to leave one chastened and humble, deeply aware of one's limitless capacity for self-deception, pretense, and cant. But at the same time there is an accumulated sense of one's viability beyond all of that; beneath all the narcissistic strategies, beneath all the constituent elements of one's identity there is an imageless abiding in God, a sense of God's pervading Presence that, as Samuel Terrien has expressed it, though it disappears is experienced "as an absence which has been overcome."[19]

It is this aspect of the apophatic tradition that is most pertinent to our postmodern situation. The sociology of knowledge, following on the heels of Nietzsche, Freud, and Marx, has brought us to an understanding that all structures of the knowledge of reality are rooted ultimately in unprovability and sustained by consensus of the social group affirming them. The apophatic tradition has always known of the imperfection of our will and intellect, our penchant for self-deception, the reliance on social reinforcement of our identity and ideology. The apophatic tradition has warned us to detach ourselves from dependence on all forms of thought and social appropriation, which function to intrude between ourselves and God.

Apophatic spirituality is marked by a deep sense of participation in God, or of the Presence and immanence of God, and yet also by a sense of God's mystery, the utter transcendence and ultimate unknowability of God per se. Urban Holmes evokes this as he writes, "There is an infinite presence of the not-yet-known that engages the horizon of our knowing and yet recedes before our inquiry into infinite mystery."[20]

The notion of God's transcendence, by itself, can be part of a very intellectualized faith; it can lead to a depersonalized orientation to the divine in which God becomes a distant, unknowable principle of coherence, or first cause. What characterizes the apophatic theology and spirituality of the Eastern and Russian traditions, however, is the sense of intense, intimate, personal relationship, the sense of God's immanence.

This is made possible by the notion of the heart, which George Maloney describes as "the center of man's spirit where man can communicate and surrender himself totally in love to God. It is the 'place' where I take my life in hand and fashion it for good or evil into what I wish myself to become."[21] Vladimir Lossky describes it as "the highest part of the human creature, . . . that contemplative faculty by which man is able to seek God."[22]

Theophan the Recluse taught, "You seek the Lord? Seek, but only within yourself. He is not far from anyone. The Lord is near all those who truly call on Him. Find a place in your heart, and speak there with the Lord. It is the Lord's reception room. Everyone who meets the Lord, meets Him there. He has fixed no other place for meeting souls."[23] Elsewhere Theophan says, "Stand in the heart, with the faith that God is also there, but *how* He is there do not speculate. Pray and entreat that in due time love for God may stir within you by His grace."[24]

The repetition of the Jesus Prayer followed by the wordless, imageless movement of the mind or consciousness toward the heart brings about a relentless encounter with one's own personhood. And along with that—experienced as graced—there happens from time to time an awareness of the Presence apprehended, not thought or imagined, of Another.

Apprehended, knowable, but not definable, the how beyond our accounting for—the Presence of the One present in Scripture and tradition happens. Although spatial images are not adequate for this dimension of experience, nevertheless, because one is in silent solitude, searching deeply toward one's center, the language of interiority is inevitable. And therefore the sense of intimate participation in the Presence happens, which enables the personal sense of immanence that is in tension with the apprehension and conviction of God's transcendence.

Thomas Merton has described such moments as "the metaphysical intuition of Being ... an intuition of a *ground of openness* ... infinite generosity that communicates itself to everything that is. 'The good is diffusive itself,' or 'God is love.' ... There is also a non-metaphysical way of stating this. It does not consider God either as Immanent or Transcendent but as grace and presence, hence neither as a 'center' imagined somewhere 'out there' nor 'within ourselves.' It encounters Him not as Being but as Freedom and Lord."[25] Merton goes on to say that these two ways should not be opposed but be seen as expressing or approaching the same awareness in different ways.

Psychologically informed pastors may wonder what is the relation between the dynamics of this centering/apophatic approach to prayer and the psychological processes they are wanting to enable in their people. First of all, centering procedures have the overall effect of relaxation and thereby function as an antidote to stress and anxiety. Persons report that after twenty minutes of centering they feel more "together," less fragmented, more of a piece. Headaches and muscular tension often disappear. Dr. Herbert Benson's book *The Relaxation Response* documents some of the long-range physiological benefits of a centering type of meditation process he uses with hypertension patients.[26]

Centering procedures can give anxious and obsessive persons a way of breaking the repetitive thinking that so troubles them. The instructions of the meditation enable them to turn their attention away from these thoughts for a time. Of course, some persons are *too* anxious, and become "flooded" when they try to sit in silence like this. So pastors must use some psychological discernment before suggesting and teaching these procedures. And, of course, pastors must have worked with these procedures themselves for several months or a year before trying to instruct others, so that they will know some of the effects firsthand.

Also we are not talking about instantaneous "results" either physically, psychologically, or religiously. We are discussing a long-range discipline which must be integrated into one's daily round. As indicated in the section dealing with centering procedures, such an approach brings the person inevitably in encounter with herself or himself. This is unavoidable and integral to the process. Continual engagement with one's actual experience in this way can lead in many different directions. Simultaneously, one can develop greater basic self-acceptance and dissatisfaction with oneself.

As the Christian tradition of prayer has always known, the earliest stages of prayer are very difficult because one encounters the "demons" or "wild beasts" or "vipers" within. Resolve and commitment are crucial at this stage, to see the person through what can be a very difficult time of self-reproach, guilt, resentment, and depression. This is one reason pastors should help people begin their prayer discipline in small groups that meet together weekly or biweekly. In these small groups, people can discuss what their experience has been (not necessarily revealing the *content* of their experience). It is supportive when alone to know that one is part of a group struggling with a similar experience.

This kind of interiority is not usual for most persons in

mainline denominations. Those who think about it at all often misconstrue prayer as either simply verbal petition, or a mysterious infusion of good feeling inculcated by an esoteric technique. Thus, sitting, counting one's breath while being distracted and sometimes buffeted by one's mutinous mind can seem pointless, painful, and humiliating. People need to be carefully and supportively instructed so that they experience and are assured of the physiological benefits. The relaxation involved will help them feel more centered. But the self-encounter may defeat them if they are left alone.

It sometimes happens that what persons experience in meditation like this leads them to want not only spiritual direction but also counseling. The pastor who is taking responsibility for guidance in prayer needs to be sensitive at this point. His or her primary attention is on what is happening in these persons regarding their experience of God, feelings toward God, and their sense of their relationship to God as it is affected by and during their praying. If the pastor sees that the person's anxiety or depression continues over a period of time without the person gaining any freedom from it in meditation, then the pastor may conclude that psychological or relational conflicts need discussion in counseling. Although opinions differ among experienced directors, I think that at such a point sensitive referral to a competent counselor is advisable.

On the other hand, greater self-awareness, which can be concurrent with the deepened experience of acceptance, can be a motivating factor for some to seek counseling. This is not to be interpreted to mean that serious meditation and prayer *ought* to lead to therapy. It is not the case that self-encountering prayer functions as a conduit toward counseling. It is simply that such prayer can lead some persons to determine to explore themselves and their relationships and aims in a therapeutic context in addition to the context of their relationship to God.

The most consistent effect that I have found with this approach to prayer is that people confront their desire to glean from God various compensations and reassurances reflective of a childish relation to a parental deity. The centering and apophatic approach to prayer involves both an encounter with one's own identity and with one's desire to control God. One's own identity includes many elements: pride in one's intellect, sense of purpose and commitment, capacity for empathy, guilt feelings, feelings of inferiority, ability to solve problems, sense of humor, resentments, ambitions, aesthetic sensitivity, and business acumen. In our relations with others, and with ourselves, we rely on these ways of experiencing ourselves to tell us who we are and remind us *that* we are. In the language of the tradition, we are "attached" to them. They are our interior possessions which also possess us because the threat of the loss of them is experienced as the threat of the loss of self.

Our relationship to God inevitably includes the transference onto God of the expectations for personal identity, reward, and punishment by which we know ourselves in interaction with others, and harking back to our relationships with those to whom we were most closely attached and upon whom we were initially dependent. When we are deprived of those means of wresting reinforcement from others or from God, then we tend to become depressed, angry, and/or anxious. Thus in this kind of prayer, we come face to face with the many ways we do not trust that we are accepted just as we are. While we can acknowledge our acceptance intellectually, in prayer we discover that our inability to trust that acceptance is, indeed, our state.

Here we have the coming together of several elements alluded to in the process of describing centering and apophatic prayer. First, the centering procedure enables increased self-awareness, and, therefore, a greater degree of integration of personality, as one needs less and less to close off portions of oneself from awareness. This also involves greater self-acceptance, and simultaneously incremental detachment from identification with specific aspects of oneself, as the instructions for letting go of all distractions affect the degree of attachment to larger configurations of aspects of one's identity.

There begins to develop an awareness of one's own "depth" "beneath" all the configurations of identity, a kind of fullness of potentiality empty of specific "content," which is experienced as the source of foundation or grounding for one's psychosocial self. Gradually there develops a confidence and trust in this depth, one's own presence to oneself.

In part by analogy and in part simply simultaneously, one becomes increasingly appreciative of and apprehensive of God as beyond anything that can be said or thought about God—a sense of the infinite "isness" of God. This enables persons to become less attached to particular formulations about God, and thereby able to appreciate and respond to various ways of describing and experiencing God, various traditional symbolic representations of the divine, knowing that there is another mode of being different from what can be symbolized and is available within human language.

This dimension of experience is pointed to by the third referent of "spirit" mentioned in chapter 2, and designated in the Orthodox tradition as both "heart" and "spirit." It will be recalled that this dimension of the person is not identified with one's character, or identity, or ego, "still less," in Merton's words, "with the neurotic or narcissistic self."[27] Merton says, "The *identity* or the *person* which is the subject of this transcendent consciousness is not the ego as isolated and contingent, but the person as 'found' and 'actualized' in union with Christ."[28] Christ and Spirit are the Christian symbols that express what is known in these unifying moments. But the knower is not the ego-subject; the knower and the known are one. This one, spirit-Spirit, is the ultimate ground of our contingent self.

Here we can appreciate the importance of Trinitarian symbolism for spirituality. We might say that God gives him/herself to be known in many ways: as Creator, Presence, Rock-and-Redeemer; in Jesus; in the Presence known as Jesus the Christ; as sustaining, transforming power, as nurturing Spirit. The doctrine of the Trinity—in its many articulations—attempts to express and account for the fact that human beings experience themselves as created by, encountered by, addressed by, saved by, sustained by, transformed by, participating in, and unified with the Divine. And in all these different moments of experience, with their different qualifications, it is still the One God who is known. In the Christian tradition this religious perception is symbolized by God, Jesus, Christ, Logos, Spirit, Father, Son, Holy Ghost, Creator, Redeemer, Sustainer. The doctrine of the Trinity implicitly recognizes that human spirituality, and Christian spirituality, are diverse and pluralistic. We do not and cannot live only in the realm of mystical union. We live in a created world of nature and of relationships, of joy and of suffering. We live as ego-subjects with a given character structure and identity. We, therefore, need God to have a human face, and we need to experience person-to-person relationship as grounded in ultimacy. These reflections, of course, relate only to the function of the doctrine of the Trinity for Christians' spirituality. They say nothing about the relationship among the persons of the Trinity. This latter is a subject for metaphysical speculation and/or mystical intuition beyond this writer's accomplishment.

But we *do* live as ego-subjects in a world of complexity and relationships, of consternations, anxiety, anger, and joy. And as Christians we believe that God has both created and entered this world and continues to transform it and us. Awareness of this in immediacy is what is pointed to by the symbol Presence. One purpose of prayer is the enhancement of our awareness of God's Presence in all aspects of life, in many different modes of experience, both in those focal moments of awareness while praying and in the ordinary moments of life, which become prayer as our spirituality matures in its alertness to Presence. In the next section, we will look at several different types of prayer that enrich our sense of relationship to this Trinitarian God, that can deepen our sense of openness to and participation in God's transforming process in Jesus, and Christ, and that can quicken our awareness of the sustaining nurturing Spirit. What we discover to be true about our depth we learn to be true of the depth in Being. Such apprehension of ourselves and of the context of our being creates the conditions within which we can begin to let go of some of our images of God as ultimate parent, judge, ruler, and so on. We come to know all of these as imperfect reflections of personal constructs. Parental language about God tends to reinforce elements of our personality left over from infantile psychosocial conflicts. Unsatisfied dependency needs, conditional acceptance, resentment of more powerful parents—these experiences subtly (and not so subtly) pervade our spirituality. I regard them as incompatible with mature spirituality and with mature personhood. Of course, it is unrealistic to imagine that as persons we are ever totally free of the residual effect of childhood experience; likewise, our understanding and relationship to God will always be traced with these conflicts.

Nevertheless, when our religious orientation has no other experiential base than the projection of infantile dynamics and the language that reinforces it, then personal and religious formation toward maturity is extremely difficult. The tendency is to relate to God on the basis of narcissistic deficiency or grandiosity. This truncates spiritual formation because we then manipulate the symbol to supply the psychic nutriment necessary for our felt viability.

As indicated in my paper "Merton and Freud: Beyond Oedipal Religion,"[29] I am convinced that Freud's perception of religion, augmented by the object relations approach of Ana-Marie Rizzuto[30] and Paul Pruyser,[31] brilliantly illuminates much contemporary spirituality. I also speculate that much of the withdrawal of persons from active engagement in the churches is because personally they have grown beyond such religiosity but in the churches are confronted by language and actions (and sermons) that unknowingly are preoccupied with the issues of infancy. This critique, incidentally, applies to liberal as well as more conservative churches.

Now we can see how the development of apophatic spirituality can mesh with a developed understanding of the postmodern intellectual situation. Apophatic spirituality is the essential condition for a faith that recognizes the relativity of all symbol systems and constructions of reality to the social contexts in which they function. This is not to say that none of them can be true; one or more might be true. But contemporary sociology of knowledge has demonstrated that any explanatory system can only explain within the terms of its own system, which ultimately rests on assumptions or intuitions that go beyond "provability." It is thus that experience is crucial to the religious/theological enterprise. Ultimately the coherence of a system rests upon its capacity to organize and articulate experience. And, of course, it must be able to elicit the kind of experience it functions to vindicate.

The apophatic tradition radically relativizes all language about God and thereby undermines the basis of our neurotic manipulations of God. Regular apophatic prayer keeps us deeply mindful of this, and in so doing, frees us to recover the symbolic language of our tradition as symbolic. This procedure in prayer thus provides a sustained, disciplined, experience-based process for what Paul Ricoeur has described as the recovery of "second naiveté."[32]

In the next sections, we will be describing various procedures in prayer which, when included with the apophatic disciplines just described, can enable the deepening of the encounter between ourselves and the structure of power and meaning made personal through Scripture.

The conventional understanding of prayer is of verbalized prayers of petition, intercession, thanksgiving, confession, and adoration. As we saw in the previous section, however, there is a long and strong tradition in Christianity of wordless prayer, known variously as contemplative prayer, the Prayer of Quiet, Prayer of the Heart, and so on. We will next discuss verbalized prayer, and then what will be called "imagistic" prayer.

Verbalized Prayer

For humans, verbalized expression is the primary means of communication. We use language to express what we experience and what we mean. "Word" in Judeo-Christian etymology means far more than simply a linguistic symbol. "Word" goes back to the Hebrew *davar,* which meant not only written or spoken word but also event, happening, or experience. The *davar* was the expression of the person; it had active creative power. As applied to Yahweh, the word not only went forth and accomplished, but also carried Yahweh's Presence. Human words, of course, have not the power of Yahweh's words, but our words do carry our meaning; that is, both what we want the words to mean and what our meaning as persons is.

For humans, words function in another way as well. The old joke that goes, "How do I know what I think until I've heard what I have to say?" has more than a little truth in it. Our words lead us not only toward the other for whom they are intended, but also lead us into ourselves, or rather, they draw us out. We discover ourselves with our own words. Intimacy, characterized by deep conversation, can be threatening for this reason. Our shared words lead us into ourselves and into others in ways that threaten both deep opposition and deep communion. As we fear abandonment, engulfment, and estrangement, most of us settle for superficial conversation that is limited to creating the bridge between two persons rather than functioning as highways into their heartlands.

In recent decades (and perhaps for longer) verbalized prayer has been a problem for liberal Christians. The scientific world view and philosophical critiques did not support the view of petitionary prayer as affecting either events in the sensory world or the consciousness of God to act contrary to the course of events, which are seen to have their own momentum. In addition, verbalized prayer seemed to assume the context of child to parent relationship, and viewing God as parent has seemed to perpetuate the kind of infantile religiosity that Freud so effectively analyzed. Prayers in church services are too often mindlessly heard or repeated; something gone through; seldom truly expressive of our inner meaning, except in moments of extremes of pain or pleasure. The decline of the "reasonableness" of a personal God has led to a withering away of verbalized prayer. And perhaps nothing has so furthered the loss of the sense of God as personal as our inability to pray.

The fundamental fact of this dialectical sequence of events is the loss of our attentiveness to interior experience. Our attention has turned outward to an external God and events in an external world. Or, for many, the hermeneutics of suspicion have warned us away from what might be, after all, mere projection. And our culture "knows" that events in the "external" world function according to strict cause and effect principles discerned by natural science. So, even if one "believes in" an external God, one does not expect God to intervene in the world, which now operates according to its own principles of natural law.

We have conceived of prayer as petition and persuasion or coercion, and our liberal scruples prohibited us from seeking special favors and from what seemed like manipulating God. Afraid of violating the genteel, sophisticated conditions we placed on our relationship to God, the experience of relationship quite naturally vanished into the thin air of theological affirmations.

The more sophisticated psychology of relationships, augmented by the philosophical implications of the psychology of consciousness and the sociology of knowledge, can help us understand the origin of relationship in the undifferentiated matrix of self and other, subject and external world. Consciousness is as much construct as discovery; others are as our experience enables and receives them. Consciousness is of something other, even if it in part creates what it in part perceives, experiences, and responds to.

Verbalized prayer (vocal or silent) is thus a crucial vehicle for the experience of our relationship with God. We cannot relate to God only as mysterious abyss or first principle. Because we are persons who require relationship, our religious being also requires the experience of relationship. And verbal prayer— conversation—is crucial. If we understand verbalized prayer as conversation rather than as an attempt to persuade or argue with God, then we have the foundation for relationship. But our first concern must be *not* what can I get out of it by way of met wishes, reassured feelings, instant knowledge of God's presence. Our first concern must be to be honestly present in our conversation. As Barry and O'Connell have written, our relationship with God is like every other relationship: it thrives (or doesn't) according to the degree of our being honest and present in the relationship.[33] Our first question should not be, Where is God in our praying? but, Where are we? Again, this is why learning to pay attention, through centering meditation, is crucial to all aspects of prayer and our whole relationship to God. If we cannot be attentive to our own *davar* in prayer, we are literally not participating in a relationship. Our attention *is* participation. This is what we fail to understand because we have failed, in our culture, to take inner experience seriously. Psychoanalysis has taught us to take the unconscious with great seriousness and to become in touch with our feelings, but even this tends to be more a focus on the contents rather than on the quality of our consciousness. In psychoanalysis we tend to identify with our rage or guilt or sexual longing rather than be aware of the quality of attention, which is the essential condition for all the rest.

So attention and honesty are the two essential premises of praying. In an act of construction isomorphic with every other relationship, we imagine ourselves before God, we express ourselves honestly and attentively, and forget about what we can "get out of the relationship." We must let go of instrumental, exploitative, self-serving motivation in our praying. This is never achieved once for all; such self-loss is never of long duration, and is always experienced as graced. Of course, this is itself only possible as a lifelong process.

Verbalized (again, not necessarily vocal) prayer is ambiguous, because it can so easily lead to or reinforce self-deception and projection. But we must not recoil from prayer because we cannot be assured of guiltlessness. As in any relationship, we express and understand and experience ourselves and the other inaccurately at times. As the relationship matures and deepens we get to know each other more fully and deeply. And as any truly married couple can testify, the misunderstandings and discoveries and otherness both of oneself and the other deepen and become more complex as the relationship matures. In a significant human relationship, the two partners do in fact create each other as they discover each other. Therefore, we need not relate to God as to preformed, adamantine personhood. Both the prophets and the process theologians remind us of God's pathos and vulnerability, God's own becoming in relationship to creation, and this means also to us as persons.

In a significant relationship, conversation emerges from and is surrounded by silence. Indeed silence is essential as preparation and for receptiveness to words. God's *davar* to us is seldom verbal in our sense. We can "hear" God only as we are attentive and receptive in an inner silence. If we cannot be silent to ourselves we cannot experience that inner event which is both God's *davar* to us and our response to God.

It should be clear, then, how enabling persons to develop this kind of capacity for praying is in continuity with pastoral care that sees the facilitation of persons' growth in capacity for relationship as close to the heart of the vocation. Prayer, as the context of relationship with God, can be formative quite as powerfully as marriage counseling, individual counseling, or group interaction. But in all the others we may miss the dimension of that primary relatedness to God. Further, prayer as we have described it is clearly in continuity with that aspect of pastoral care that is concerned with world-construction and maintenance. For prayer is the means by which we know ourselves not only in principle subject to the cosmos, but as personally related to its essential heart. Again, the place of experience is central.

Pastors who wish to help their people grow in capacity for prayer of the sort have several resources. First, of course, is their own development in prayer. Unless the pastor experiences such prayerfulness she or he will not be of much help to parishioners. A pastor's counseling should be marked by the capacity for empathic listening that grows out of the pastor's own capacity to be open to his or her own feelings and the ability to disclose them appropriately to others. This is foundational to prayer also. Therefore, as the pastor facilitates others' self-disclosure in counseling, so the pastor can encourage persons to open their hearts to God in the context of prayer.

For some people, this may seem artificial or contrived at first. Again, this is why the first thing to be taught in the development of prayer life is centering. This, again, helps persons to be more receptive to their own inwardness, and to develop the alternate state of consciousness that is more appropriate for conversation with God than our ordinary day-to-day consciousness. Beginners may be encouraged to spend fifteen to twenty minutes in centering, and then to read a psalm slowly, aloud or to oneself, as if it were one's own prayer. Many psalms can be experienced as startlingly appropriate personally once the reader understands that his or her own perplexities, pains, resentments, joys, guilts, and anxieties are themselves the stuff of prayer life.

For example, notice the themes of guilt, despair, anger, and depression in Psalm 6 of the Jerusalem Bible. How close it is to genuine personal experience; especially, I think, those struggling with the predictable stresses of aging would discover inner resonance to its words.

> Yahweh, do not punish me in your rage
> or reprove me in the heat of anger.
> Pity me, Yahweh, I have no strength left,
> heal me, my bones are in torment,
> my soul is in utter torment.
> Yahweh, how long will you be?
>
> Come back, Yahweh, rescue my soul,
> save me, if you love me;
> for in death there is no remembrance of you:
> who can sing your praises in Sheol?
>
> I am worn out with groaning,
> every night I drench my pillow
> and soak my bed with tears;
> my eye is wasted with grief,
> I have grown old with enemies all round me.
>
> Away from me, all you evil men!
> For Yahweh has heard the sound of my weeping;
> Yahweh has heard my petition,
> Yahweh will accept my prayer.
> Let all my enemies, discredited, in utter torment,
> fall back in sudden confusion.

(JB)

This is strong stuff. Some persons feel that one ought not let oneself feel these feelings, let alone express them to God. They are not pious, they are "negative," not upbeat, and even vengeful. But they are *honest.* Informed by the life cycle theory of Erik Erikson, pastors know that the stages of life are marked by predictable vicissitudes and conflicts that, unless worked through, will leave the person with reduced capacity for self-affirmation and strong engagement with others. And, instructed by the approach to counseling of Carl Rogers, contemporary pastors know of the healing that occurs when one is able to express one's inner experience in the presence of one who listens and understands and accepts.

One of the virtues of the Jerusalem Bible's version of the Psalms is its use of the very personal name, Yahweh. This heightens the sense of being in actual conversation, in a personal relationship. The words "Lord" and "God" seem more distancing and impersonal to many contemporaries. But part of Christian spirituality has been the sense that Ultimate Reality is in some sense personal at its center, that the I-Thou dimension of experience is neither fiction nor projection. Christian spirituality must regain this truth.

Another psalm that expresses feelings many can identify with, if they are open to their own experience, is Psalm 69:

Save me, God! The Water
is already up to my neck!

I am sinking in the deepest swamp,
there is no foothold;
I have stepped into deep water
and the waves are washing over.

Worn out with calling, my throat is hoarse,
my eyes are strained, looking for my God.

(JB)

Every pastor, harried businessperson, or anyone who has had to balance job and family responsibilities can identify with the anxiety of being overwhelmed by responsibilities and ex-pectations. The metaphors of water and swamp are apt also for the flood of feelings that can result from essentially intra-psychic conflict, as well. Helpful also in this psalm is the honest articulation that throughout all of this, God seems uncon-cerned and elsewhere. Mature Christian spirituality has always known the reality of the experience of God's absence. It is spiritually healing in itself just to know that one can be sus-tained even in the midst of the experience of desolation and abandonment.

One final, well-known example from the psalms is Psalm 139. No other psalm (and few pieces of religious expression anywhere) can equal the breadth and depth of the experience of God's presence expressed in this psalm. And even in this psalm, though usually expunged from lectionaries, there is an upsurge of vengeful self-justification. However out of keeping with the overall sense of the psalm, the eruption of these "negative" feelings is utterly authentic psychologically. Any-one who has experienced uncritical awareness of their flow of feeling will recognize that such intrusions are the way our psyches work. This is one of the lessons from a discipline that enables honesty in prayer, that we experience all sorts of un-predictable feelings. But it is also the case that developing honesty in prayer can reveal capacities for love and compassion and comprehension we may have long denied to our aware-ness.

A resource similar to the psalms is that of the hymnal. Said or read as prayers, many of our well-known hymns are marvelous vehicles for spiritual expression and formation. Such hymns as "When I Survey the Wondrous Cross" and "My Faith Looks Up to Thee" lead one deeper into the apprehension of the meaning of the person of Jesus; that is, simply put, as our person becomes more open in response to Jesus, Jesus be-comes more personal to us.

Imagistic Prayer

In this type of prayer, images, rather than words, are the vehicle of expression. For example, a pastor might be concerned about an important meeting with the governing board of the church. In prayer, the pastor might verbalize whatever concerns he or she has about the purpose and outcome of the meeting, the persons involved, and the dynamics he or she expects, hopes for, or is apprehensive about. Included in the prayer might be a petition for courage, wisdom, or patience, as well as for a positive outcome.

Praying imagistically would be different. In this kind of prayer, the pastor would first spend fifteen to twenty minutes in centering prayer. As described above, this would help to focus the attention away from the various distractions of the daily round, physically relax one, and prepare one for responsiveness to inner experience rather than to the various claims and agendas of the outer world. Such centering also helps one to be more alert, more keenly attentive to the events of inner experience, more readily attuned to subtleties and nuance of feeling and response.

Gradually, one lets oneself picture in one's mind the scene of the meeting. One visualizes the room and its physical arrangement and appearance, being attentive to the details of the scene. Then one pictures the person coming into the meeting and taking their places around the table. One pictures each person, letting one's imagination dwell on each person in turn. In this process one is attentive not only to the person but to one's own reactions to the person visualized. One does not try to achieve any particular kind of feelings about each person, but only tries to let oneself be open to what one's actual experience of each person is.

This is a basic step in prayer, being open and honest about who one is. Pretense simply reinforces defensive structures and severely limits the possibilities of experience and response in situations and relationships. In this approach, the receptive mode replaces the active mode of ordinary consciousness; and being receptive to one's actual experience tends to develop a kind of humility as well as appreciation of one's own actuality. One develops the capacity to receive oneself as one is; and, of course, this is necessary for being able to receive others.

The process of noticing one's responses to each person and letting the feelings go after noticing them facilitates two complementary and correlated processes. One is the development of what ego psychologists would call the "observing ego." That is, one develops a capacity to be aware of oneself and observe one's feelings but not be totally enmeshed in them. The correlate process is what the tradition has called (as we have seen) "detachment." Letting the feelings go reduces one's identification with them. One knows oneself apart from these specific feelings and reactions. This does *not* mean that one no longer cares, or that one becomes invulnerable. It simply means that one develops a firmer sense of one's own viability, as not being bound to any accumulated structure of response to persons or situations. Development of the observing ego enhances a sense of a center not controlled by feelings stirred up by others, which in the end are ego-defensive or narcissistically gratifying.

As the praying pastor images each person, in this receptive and attentive state, more "response-information" becomes available to the pastor. That is, one is able to become aware of more facets, more dimensions of these people than when one is caught up on one's agenda-orientation toward them. In these agenda-oriented transactions, one's attention is likely to be more on what one wants from the transaction or on how others are impacting one in the transaction than on being open and receptive to their fullness as persons. This broader receptivity to others enables one to experience their participation in the meeting in the broader context of their being as persons.

One then might let oneself visualize the discussion that might take place around one or more significant issues. Again, one's mental state is one of receptivity, of letting the scene unfold rather than of controlling each step. Knowing the persons involved, one has some idea of how each might begin to address the issue. One can just let the conversation begin and then let the persons take their parts.

This may sound contrived. And the first few times one works this way in prayer, one may feel that it is artificial, that one is simply putting words in persons' mouths. Serious prayer *is* a different kind of endeavor of the mind than we are used to; it takes practice to become simultaneously attentive and receptive to the flow of inner images.

But over time one finds that such a process enables one to experience different facets of the persons involved and different reactions and responses of one's own. The "mind" is a constructive resource of much more "information" than we are ordinarily aware of. This imagistic process enables us to be more receptive to more of it. New insight, new understanding, new possibilities can occur as we open ourselves receptively in this kind of prayer.

The reader might be wondering what makes this imaging exercise "prayer." It may seem similar to what goes on in psychological counseling, or some types of Jungian therapy, or even daydreaming. First, its similarity to other procedures obviously does not disqualify a procedure as prayer. Otherwise, verbalized prayer itself would not qualify. But, the response might be, in verbalized prayer the object of address is God, whereas in imagistic prayer there is no address to God; it is just something we are doing inside our own heads.

This, of course, raises significant theological issues. It illustrates why a notion of God that is rooted in the Cartesian structure of the separation of subject and object leads to the loss of experienced religion. It is essential that we recover language about God that helps to undergird the sense of God's presence in our experience. This is different from saying that God addresses us from outside and we experience God's Word. Rather, what is called for is a recovery of the sense of God's immanence to our experience, what Paul was driving at when he wrote of the Spirit praying through our spirit.

John Cobb is striving for this in his writing about "directivity."[34] Cobb describes directivity as "more mysterious and elusive than form or matter, . . . not manifest in inorganic things, . . . although incipiently it may be present in the particles that make these up. But in living things and in human experience it is . . . an orientation toward the future, an aim, a directionality, a goal-directedness."[35]

If one believes that God is actively, immanently present, sustaining all things, nudging and luring them toward the greatest fulfillment possible under given conditions, then it becomes incumbent upon us to discern as fully as possible what these conditions actually are and to let ourselves be aligned with the creative possibilities toward which this "directivity" can lead us. And clearly, our consciousness, our attitudes, our defensiveness, our hope, our experience of others, are all part of the given condition of a situation. Imagistic prayer is one way of our letting ourselves become more open to the range of reality of a given situation, in the faith and expectation that in so doing we are led to greater wholeness within the situation, greater sensitivity to the actuality of it, and greater responsiveness to its possibilities for good.

This approach to prayer moves away from the notion of the separation of grace and nature. It does not assume that prayer is answered by some infusion of quasi-substantial grace. Rather, the created processes of the human are themselves graced, the expression of what the early Fathers called the "energies" of God.[36] Elucidating the work of Gregory Palamas, George Maloney paraphrases him: "Man must open himself to God's uncreated energies that are always 'gracing' man at every moment in each event."[37] But this is not a grace "added to" or contravening nature. Rather, the experience of grace is the heightened responsiveness to all processes of life as expressive of the immanence of God, present through God's "energies."

The approach to prayer and spirituality developed in this book emphasizes both God's ultimate unknowableness and an ever-deepening apprehension of oneself-in-relation-to-God. Likewise, although praying may be a distinct activity in itself, and at times will be without any images or connectedness to "ordinary" life, yet all of our life becomes incorporated in our praying: all of our concerns, our hopes, our relationships, our anxieties, and our projects are experienced in prayer, in a time of heightened awareness of ourselves before God. And then we move from this mode of experiencing into our lives in the world with greater openness to how God's "energies" may be active there as well as in our praying.

In the movement from our praying to the world, renewed and reconstituted by our participation in liturgy and the community, our spirituality develops its shape and color. *How* we experience these moments and this movement, and how we express our experience and integrate it with our words and actions, *is* our spirituality. This understanding of spirituality affirms our calling to participate in the ongoing, creative, transforming action of God in the world, and to vivify our experience of and, finally, our love of God.

The example of imagistic praying described above is oriented toward a life situation. It is an approach to prayer drawn from Saint Ignatius of Loyola, who relied a great deal on the process of visualization. He did not limit visualization to life situations, but also invited the exercitant to image dialogue with the persons of the Trinity, or the Blessed Virgin and other personages; in addition, he prescribed imagistic prayer visualizing spiritual battles and other nonearthly events. And it is to Ignatius that we turn for an approach to working with Scripture in prayer, utilizing our capacity for imaging.

Let us take, for example, the story of Jesus calming the storm, in the Gospel of Mark. As in the previous example, the one praying spends some time in centering, then lets the scene of the story come to mind. The scene by the lakeside is visualized, the attention being focused on the sights, sound, smells, objects, persons, and the landscape. The idea is that the scene is to become vivid in its particulars, as if the person were there, experiencing it. Just as centering helps prepare for this kind of prayer, so attending to these details of sensation helps to bring the one praying bodily into the event of the story.

The person imagines a group walking down the beach; among them is Jesus. The one praying then visualizes oneself joining the group, noticing the persons there, listening to what they are discussing, and observing both Jesus and one's own reaction to the scene. Then the person imagines each segment of the story as clearly as possible, with oneself involved in the action. In the process one pays attention both to the action to one's reaction to one's experience, especially one's reaction to Jesus.

After this, the one praying lets one's mind cast about in one's current life, and then asks the question: What is the storm in my life, or what storm is brewing in my life? Then one lets oneself experience this storm in imagination, picturing all the aspects of it, all the relationships involved, all the conflicts, the possibilities, the values at stake. In this process the emphasis is on the *experience* of these elements, not on rational, analytical thought about them. When one has accomplished this, then one images oneself discussing this with Jesus, calling on Jesus to be present amidst one's storm, or telling Jesus whatever one wants to about one's experience of the storm in one's life. This is what Saint Ignatius calls a colloquy.

By now, the reader is familiar with the principles and dynamics of imagistic prayer. Experiencing the story as it is told by Mark brings one into encounter with the biblical Jesus and the reaction of the followers to him. The dynamics of the story are enabled to energize one's sense of one's own life situation by using the story metaphorically as one becomes aware of one's own life "storm." Being still in a physically relaxed, centered, attentive, and receptive state of consciousness, one's defenses are somewhat reduced, one's "automatized" reactions are somewhat neutralized so that more of one's experience can come into awareness.

Finally, the colloquy sets up an encounter with Jesus that one may experience with some personal vividness. Of course, the beginner may well experience this as somewhat contrived, as "putting words into Jesus' mouth." But one man doing this the first time found that Jesus did not want to discuss the "storm" he had selected. Jesus wanted to discuss the man's relationship with his child, which the man had been successfully not thinking about during the meditation but which in fact was a source of much conflict and pain in his life.

A common reaction for many is to discover that in the boat during the storm they feel anger toward Jesus, an unacceptable emotion for many. The experience of the storm in the story makes it possible for some persons who tend to deny their feelings to be more in touch with their actual feelings when they imagine the storm in their own life. This then makes them more at one with themselves, more of a piece, since they are no longer unaware of these feelings. Being more aware of one's feelings, one then has more "information" about the meaning of a given situation, and therefore has more complete information to bring to bear on whatever decisions or actions need to be taken. Of course, in some cases no decision or action can be taken; one simply has to endure the situation. In this case the prayer may help one experience the sustaining presence of Jesus, or one may become aware that one has no vivid feelings about Jesus' involvement in one's life. This is an equally important lesson for the process of spiritual formation.

The man who wanted to avoid his conflict with his child was quite startled by the apparently autonomous "initiative" exercised by the figure of Jesus. He did not feel that he had "put words into Jesus' mouth" nor did he feel the interaction was contrived, as so often happens when persons begin working in prayer in this way and still are reacting in an "automatized" way.

The lowered anxiety of the relaxed meditative state, the focused attention, and the altered state of consciousness that results all function to enable the surfacing of the central problem in a person's life and relationship, which this man had been avoiding. In his prayer situation of physical relaxation and lowered anxiety, the figure of Jesus, functioning as an element of both superego and ego ideal, was able to overcome the denial tendencies and mobilize that part of his intentionality that wanted to come to grips with the relationship. While a "solution" was not found, the man's resistance to working on the problem was crucially reduced. He now felt mobilized and able to deal with the problem.

Obviously, this exercise does not "stand alone." It is not an experience isolated from contributing structures of value and meaning. This was a well-intentioned parent who took parental responsibility seriously. He had a mildly authoritarian personality and related to God and Jesus as authority figures. He believed that effective parenting requires openness and dialogue, even though that was not the way he was brought up; therefore, it was somewhat threatening to him. His religious community, in which he was a lay leader, places a high value on strong family relationships and sees its religion as sanctioning and supporting this.

Thus his self-esteem was threatened by his avoidance of

a family problem, and his failure to deal with that would threaten to lower his esteem in the eyes of his community of primary reference.

It is important to emphasize the social context as well as the context of the overall meaning and value system, because prayer does not occur in a privatized vacuum. Our consciousness is formed and sustained in a social context, and religious experience will have reference to that context as well as to the individual psychodynamics of the person praying. Also important is the fact that this experience occurred in a group context, and the man could experience the support and encouragement of the group to work on the relationship.

The foregoing is one example of why these directives for imagistic prayer include no instructions about how one is to feel or react, no instructions about what one is to have Jesus do or say. Such instructions are counterproductive, since they sustain our need to feel in control and they feed off the misapprehension that we know ahead of time what we *ought* to be experiencing. This vitiates the possibility of growth through prayer, even though it may result in persons "feeling better." Such approaches to prayer differ little from autosuggestion. Autosuggestion may be useful at times, but it retains control, it does not let one trust into the actuality of one's inner life, and therefore attempts to heal by suppression rather than by insight and transformation.

Such openness in prayer can gradually begin to carry over into our ordinary life, and then there can develop the synergy that marks maturing spirituality, in which our experience in prayer and our actions in the world reflect and influence each other. The key to this whole process is the concept of attentive receptivity. In the terms of Gerald May's brilliant book *Will and Spirit*,[38] we begin to let go of our willfulness and let emerge a greater capacity for willingness. We let a situation unfold rather than rush to dominate and control it.

In the deeply receptive state of consciousness of prayer, the automatization that reinforces our basic personality structure is altered by virtue of the centering attention. This permits a freer flow of imagery, feelings, and perceptions than is ordinarily the case in our waking state. The combination of centered attention on the subject of prayer (Bible story, person, situation) and a freer flow of imagery stimulated by this subject permits a broader range of "information" about our life to become conscious. This may permit a reorganization of the information and our reaction to it, so that a new solution to a life problem may emerge. Or perhaps we may discover new ways of experiencing or understanding it so that our basic stance toward it is enhanced.[39] Correlated with this experience is a deepened appreciation and awareness of God both as active love and the ultimate context of our lives.

A similar willingness should characterize our pastoral counseling. Effective pastoral counseling requires the capacity to listen accurately and acceptingly. We cannot do this if we are paying attention to our own ideas, to what we are going to say next, or to what the person ought to be feeling or doing. Accurate empathy requires attentive receptivity. When the counselor is experienced as accurately empathic and accepting and open to his or her own feelings, then healing is likely to occur. The same holds true for the process of prayer. Therefore, the dynamics of a mature prayer life share many characteristics with effective pastoral care and counseling. But the solitude of prayer generates special power, because, as Cobb has written, "With others there are always intervening variables to honesty, but thinking of oneself as alone before God enables and causes us to take a deeper responsibility for ourselves."[40] Enabling others in a mature prayer life should be seen as close to the core of pastoral care. This perception of pastoral care is sustained by a theological perspective that does not separate God from our intrapersonal dynamics toward wholeness, but affirms God's "directivity" therein as in our interpersonal encounters, and in the ongoing creating and sustaining processes of nature and history, of which persons are an integral part. This perspective does not maintain that we are always at one with this directivity, this lure toward the good; the cross is, after all, central to our religious understanding. But this perspective does affirm that a discipline can lead to greater awareness of as well as alignment with these energies of God.

For ongoing spirituality, the importance of prayer is not in the isolated experiences alone. At least as important is the cumulative effect of opening ourselves in this way. Some experience this process as God in a very personalistic way leading them into deeper self-awareness and self-acceptance, and their relationships toward honesty and harmony. Others may experience a sense of awe at how it all works, and at the ultimate graciousness of the human process and the life process in which it participates and which it exemplifies. The apprehension of God may not be so personalistic but rather a sense of living within an active process characterized ultimately by compassion and wisdom. Such awareness also encompasses a deepened comprehension of conflict, pain, and evil. The sense of God is not the feeling of avuncular indulgence. One becomes intensely aware that there are structures of Reality that when violated react ruthlessly; and, to deepen the mystery, the reality of absurd and arbitrary suffering is burned into one's sensitivity. None of this occurs overnight; it is an ongoing process of formation of the spirit, the awareness and responsiveness of the person before and within the transcendent and immanent mystery of God.

Notes

1. THE CULTURAL AND RELIGIOUS CONTEXT OF CONTEMPORARY PASTORAL CARE

1. Peter Berger, *The Sacred Canopy* (Garden City, N.Y.: Doubleday Anchor Books, 1969), 107.
2. Ibid.
3. Ibid., 108.
4. Following is a selection of works that the reader may find useful in pursuing these issues: Ian G. Barbour, *Myths, Models and Paradigms* (New York: Harper & Row, 1974); Fritjof Capra, *The Tao of Physics* (New York: Bantam Books, 1977); Lawrence LeShan, *Alternate Realities* (New York: Evans, 1975); Lawrence LeShan and Hans Margenau, *Einstein's Space and Van Gogh's Sky* (New York: Macmillan Co., 1982); Jacob Needleman, *A Sense of the Cosmos* (New York: Doubleday & Co., 1975); Robert Ornstein, *The Psychology of Consciousness* (New York: Harcourt Brace Jovanovich, 1977); Michael Polanyi, *Personal Knowledge* (New York: Harper & Row, 1964); Theodore Roszak, *The Making of a Counter Culture* (Garden City, N.Y.: Doubleday Anchor Books, 1969); Harold K. Schilling, *The New Consciousness in Science and Religion* (Philadelphia: United Church Press, 1973); Daniel Yankelovitch and William Barrett, *Ego and Instinct* (New York: Vintage Books, 1971).
5. Peter Berger, *The Heretical Imperative* (New York: Doubleday Anchor Books, 1979).
6. Thomas Oden, *Agenda for Theology* (San Francisco: Harper & Row, 1979).
7. Paul Ricoeur, *Freud and Philosophy* (New Haven, Conn.: Yale University Press, 1970).
8. Paul Ricoeur, "Psychoanalysis and Contemporary Culture," in *The Conflict of Interpretations* (Evanston, Ill.: Northwestern University Press, 1974), 154.
9. Ricoeur, *Freud and Philosophy*, 234.
10. Ibid.

11. Louis Dupre, *The Other Dimension* (New York: Seabury Press, 1979), 13.

12. Berger, *The Heretical Imperative.*

13. Ibid., 87.

14. Ibid., 96.

15. Evelyn Underhill, *Practical Mysticism* (New York: E.P. Dutton & Co., 1943), 31.

16. Peter Berger, *A Rumor of Angels* (Garden City, N.Y.: Doubleday Anchor Books, 1970).

17. Ibid., 53.

18. Ibid., 52.

19. Underhill, *Practical Mysticism*, 32.

20. Howard Thurman, *Disciplines of the Spirit* (New York: Harper & Row, 1963), 87.

21. Ibid.

2. SPIRITUALITY AND SPIRIT

1. Jacob Needleman, *A Sense of the Cosmos* (New York: Doubleday & Co., 1975).

2. Ludwig Binswarger, "Freud and the Magna Charta of Clinical Psychiartry," in *Being in the World,* ed. and trans. Jacob Needleman (New York: Basic Books, 1963), 183.

3. Ibid., 184.

4. Erik H. Erikson, *Childhood and Society* (New York: W. W. Norton Co., 1963), 23–25.

5. Daniel Yankelovitch and William Barrett, *Ego and Instinct* (New York: Vintage Books, 1971), 400.

6. Robert White, *Ego and Reality in Psychoanalytic Theory* (New York: International Universities Press, 1963).

7. Yankelovitch and Barrett, *Ego and Instinct*, 400.

8. Anthony Sutich in *The Journal of Transpersonal Psychology* 1 (Spring 1969).

9. William James, *The Varieties of Religious Experience* (New York: New American Library, 1958), 378.

10. Charles Tart, *Transpersonal Psychologies* (New York: Harper & Row, 1975), 4.

11. John Macquarrie, *Paths in Spirituality* (New York: Harper & Row, 1972), 44.

12. Robert Ornstein, *The Nature of Human Consciousness* (San Francisco: W. H. Freeman & Co., 1973).

13. Yankelovitch and Barrett, *Ego and Instinct*, 266.

14. Ibid.

15. Ibid., 279.

16. Sigmund Freud, *Civilization and Its Discontents* (New York: W. W. Norton Co., 1961), 11ff.

17. Ibid.

18. Gerald May, *Will and Spirit* (San Francisco: Harper & Row, 1982).

19. Carl Jung, *The Psychology of Religion* (New Haven: Yale University Press, 1938), 4.

20. Timothy Ware, *The Art of Prayer* (London: Faber and Faber, 1976), 21.

21. Thomas Merton, *Contemplative Prayer* (Garden City, N.Y.: Doubleday & Co., 1971), 33.

22. Urban T. Holmes, *Spirituality for Ministry* (San Francisco: Harper & Row, 1982), 12.

23. John Eusden and John Westerhoff, *The Spiritual Life: Learning East and West* (New York: Seabury Press, 1982), 2.

24. May, *Will and Spirit*, 22.

25. Ibid., 59.

26. Paul Jones, "A Search for Definition: Theological Options," in *Spiritual Formation Resource Packet* (Nashville: Division of Ordained Ministry, Board of Higher Education, 1982), 1.

3. A THEORY OF PASTORAL CARE

1. Robert N. Bellah, *Beyond Belief* (New York: Harper & Row, 1970), 21.

2. Suzanne Langer, *Philosophy in a New Key* (New York: New American Library, 1951).

3. Clifford Geertz, "Religion as a Cultural System," in *The Interpretation of Cultures* (New York: Basic Books, 1973), 93–94.

4. Andrew Greeley, *Ecstasy: A Way of Knowing* (Englewood Cliffs, N.J.: Prentice-Hall, 1974).

5. Ernest Becker, *The Heroics of Living and Dying*, Psychology Today Cassette, 1974.

6. *The Cloud of Unknowing* (Baltimore: Penguin Books, 1974), 54.

7. Readers familiar with Philip Rieff's work will recognize the tension between the terms. I favor "constriction" rather than Rieff's term "restraint" because I believe that too often an inappropriate constriction rather than disciplined restraint has been the tendency of religion. I refer the interested reader to Philip Rieff, *The Triumph of the Therapeutic* (New York: Harper & Row, 1966).

8. John Wesley, quoted in *Umphrey Lee, John Wesley and Modern Religion* (Nashville: Cokesbury Press, 1936), 107–8. Cited by Douglas Stere, *Dimension of Prayer* (New York: Board of Missions, Methodist Church, 1962), 25–27.

9. William Clebsch and Charles Jaekle, *Pastoral Care in Historical Perspective* (New York: Harper & Row, 1964), 5.

10. Howard Clinebell, *Growth Counseling for Marriage Enrichment* (Philadelphia: Fortress Press, 1975), 2.

11. Don S. Browning, *The Moral Context of Pastoral Care* (Philadelphia: Westminster Press, 1976), 21.

12. James Fowler, *Stages of Faith* (San Francisco: Harper & Row, 1981).

13. Kenneth Leach, *Soul Friend* (San Francisco: Harper & Row, 1977); Tilden Edwards, *Spiritual Friend* (New York: Paulist Press, 1980); William A. Barry and William J. Connolly, *The Practice of Spiritual Direction* (New York: Seabury Press, 1982).

14. Joe Wilson, "Nurture and Spiritual Formation of the Laity through Pastoral Care Ministry" (D.Min. diss., Drew University, 1983).

4. THE FUNCTION OF PRAYER IN SPIRITUAL FORMATION

1. Caryl Marsh, "A Framework for Describing Subjective States of Consciousness," in Norman Earl Zinberg, ed., *Alternate States of Consciousness* (New York: Free Press, 1977), 125.

2. Robert Ornstein, *The Psychology of Consciousness* (New York: Harcourt Brace Jovanovich, 1977), 44.

3. Ibid., 43.

4. Jerome C. Bruner and C. C. Goodman, "Value and Need as Organizing Factors in Perception," *Journal of Abnormal and Social Psychology* 74 (1967): 1–36. Quoted in Ornstein, *Psychology of Consciousness*, 65.

5. John C. Cobb, *To Pray or Not to Pray* (Nashville: Upper Room Publications, 1974), 24.

6. Ibid.

7. Evelyn Underhill, *Practical Mysticism* (New York: E. P. Dutton & Co., 1943).

8. St. Teresa of Avila, *The Interior Castle*, trans. E. Allison Peers (Garden City, N.Y.: Image Books, 1961), 41.

9. Thomas Merton, *Contemplative Prayer* (Garden City, N.Y.: Image Books, 1971), 24.

10. *The Way of a Pilgrim*, trans. R. M. French (New York: Ballantine Books, 1974).

11. George A. Maloney, S.J., *The Prayer of the Heart* (Notre Dame, Ind.: Ave Maria Press, 1981), 139–40.

12. Henri Nouwen, *The Way of the Heart* (New York: Seabury Press, 1981), 76.

13. Igumen Chariton, *The Art of Prayer*, trans. E. Kadloubovsky and G.E.H. Palmer (London: Faber & Faber, 1976), 71.

14. *The Cloud of Unknowing* (Baltimore: Penguin Books, 1974), 60.

15. Chariton, *Art of Prayer,* 80.

16. Ibid., 110.

17. *Cloud of Unknowing,* 61.

18. Ibid.

19. Samuel Terrien, *The Elusive Presence* (New York: Harper & Row, 1978), 476.

20. Urban T. Holmes, *Spirituality for Ministry* (New York: Harper & Row, 1982), 14.

21. George Maloney, S.J., *Inward Stillness* (Denville, N.J.: Dimension Books, 1976), 24.

22. Vladimir Lossky, *The Mystical Theology of the Eastern Church* (Crestwood, N.Y.: St. Vladimir's Seminary Press, 1957), 201.

23. Quoted in Chariton, *Art of Prayer,* 187.

24. Ibid., 191.

25. Thomas Merton, *Zen and the Birds of Appetite* (New York: New Directions, 1968), 24–25.

26. Herbert Benson, M.D., *The Relaxation Response* (New York: William Morrow, 1975).

27. Thomas Merton, *Zen and the Birds of Appetite,* 75.

28. Ibid.

29. Nelson S. T. Thayer, "Merton and Freud: Beyond Oedipal Religion," *The Journal of Pastoral Care* 35 (March 1982).

30. Ana-Marie Rizzuto, M.D., *The Birth of the Living God* (Chicago: University of Chicago Press, 1979).

31. Paul Pruyser, Ph.D., *Between Belief and Unbelief* (New York: Harper & Row, 1974).

32. Paul Ricoeur, *The Symbolism of Evil* (New York: Harper & Row, 1967), 352.

33. William Barry and William O'Connell, "Spiritual Direction: The Empirical Approach," *America* (24 April 1976): 350–58.

34. John B. Cobb, Jr., *Theology and Pastoral Care* (Philadelphia: Fortress Press, 1977), 46ff.

35. Ibid.

36. George Maloney, S.J., *A Theology of Uncreated Energies* (Milwaukee: Marquette University Press, 1978).

37. Ibid., 81.

38. Gerald May, *Will and Spirit* (San Francisco: Harper & Row, 1982).

39. For reading in the ego psychological theory that relates to this approach to prayer see the following references: Erika Fromm, "The Nature of Hypnosis and Other Altered States of Consciousness: An Ego Psychological Theory," in Erika Fromm and Ronald E. Shor, eds., *Hypnosis: Developments in Research and New Perspectives* (New York:

Aldine Publishing Co., 1979), 81–103; Arthur Deikman, "Deautomatization and the Mystic Process," in Robert Ornstein, ed., *The Nature of Human Consciousness* (San Francisco: W. H. Freeman & Co., 1973), 216–33.

40. Cobb, *To Pray or Not to Pray,* 24.